The
SEA-RINGED
WORLD

Sacred Stories
of the Americas

MARÍA GARCÍA ESPERÓN

illustrated by **AMANDA MIJANGOS**

translated by **DAVID BOWLES**

LQ

LEVINE QUERIDO

MONTCLAIR · AMSTERDAM
NEW YORK

This is an Em Querido book

Published by Levine Querido

LEVINE QUERIDO

www.levinequerido.com • info@levinequerido.com

Published September 2020

Second Printing

CONTENTS

Fifteen thousand years before Europeans stepped foot in the Americas, people had already spread from tip to tip and coast to coast. Like all humans, these Native Americans sought to understand their place in the universe, the nature of their relationship with the divine, and the origin of the world into which their ancestors had emerged.

The answers lay in their sacred stories.

Passed down through the generations, these narratives created an unbroken strand of indigenous wisdom, lore that guided life and love, warfare and worship.

When men arrived from the East in massive boats, a tragedy was set in motion that wiped out millions of souls and broad swaths of their wisdom. Some sacred stories survived, recorded in the invaders' alphabet or by the invaders' very pens. Others kept on burning like secret flames in the hearts of the original peoples. Many are recounted to this very day.

It is nearly impossible to get even a bird's-eye view of this vast if tattered lore from such a multitude of nations across the continent. What we have sought to do in these pages, however, is take up the threads of some indigenous cultures and weave a unique and varied tapestry that gives just a glimpse of their traditions.

The narratives we have collected reveal the inexorable and vast movement of generations, that endless trek from north to south, east to west, and back again. Past and present converge in these sacred tales, which speak of an original time, nearly lost and forgotten, but deeply evocative.

Some of the tales have been altered by sensibilities and languages foreign to this land, shaped by colonial mindsets and romantic notions. Wherever possible, we have tried our best to bring out the faint ancestral voices echoing at the heart of each.

Much of the wisdom these tales contain is universal. It can fit your life as easily as it did the lives of the people who heard them first. Some details will feel strange to you, out of step with what you believe to be true. Indeed, the cultures are different, not necessarily yours to emulate. And the behavior of some figures may sometimes strike you as odd or even bad. Nonetheless, there is much to be learned and treasured here. Heed the stories well.

Our hope is to open your hearts and minds to the wisdom and beauty of the people on whose land we now live. Let these vital ancient words thread themselves into the woof of your soul, teaching you to respect and admire the lore that has endured unto this moment and to weep for all that has been irrevocably lost.

Spider Grandmother

Hopi tradition

Spider Grandmother,
dearest old woman:
tell me the tale of the stars.
How the owl and the eagle fly,
why the buffalo graze and dream.

Spider Grandmother,
here in our adobe home,
your voice ensnares me:
spin your story, please!

So long ago that the years are impossible to count, a spirit lived alone in infinite space. He was surrounded by sunbeams, a halo of purest light. So much energy bubbled deep within him in his chest that he knew he must create a world. His name was Taawa, and from his hands burst forth prairies and waterfalls, an immense land full of mountains. In the midst of this world, Taawa carved a vast canyon, through which a river of crystalline waters flowed forever.

But there was no one in those beautiful lands. Taawa then had another idea: he would create a grandmother. So from his hands also emerged Kookyangwso'wuuti— Spider Grandmother. She immediately began to weave an endless web. And from that web came everything that was missing from the world that Taawa had created: clouds and fish, birds and people.

However, the nights were very dark.

Human beings set out to inhabit that first world. Spider Grandmother gave them advice, never ceasing to weave her web, to which she continuously added some new river or tree. Then down the mountains came a trickster, whose name was Iisawu—Coyote. And Muy'ingwa, a generous spirit, creator of maize.

Treating both with respect, the people lived happily until something happened in their hearts. They lost their way. They began to behave so badly that Taawa crossed his arms over his chest and his crown of sunbeams grew dark.

The people were frightened as the sky broke into pieces and the earth shook. A rain of fire fell from the clouds until a curtain of hail extinguished the flames and buried the houses. The people cried and tried to get to safety, but it was impossible. Taawa had made himself dark to destroy the world and punish the evil that had taken over the humans' hearts.

Spider Grandmother felt compassion for those few who had kept their hearts pure. She descended from her web amid the stars and led the chosen ones toward the Grand Canyon. When all had assembled, a giant, hollow reed burst from the depths of the huge fissure in the ground. Then Spider Grandmother said with a very strong voice:

"My children, the first world is over. I have woven a home for you, with beautiful meadows and blue buffalo, resplendent skies and eagles of majestic flight. That world awaits, but you must strive hard to reach it. You must climb upward inside this hollow reed that the Grand Canyon has gifted. Help one another as you go. After a long night, you will arrive at the land that I, your Spider Grandmother, have promised."

The last human beings obeyed her. They climbed up the great

reed, and at the end of the long night, they emerged through a sipaapu, a portal into their new lives. They awoke on the first morning of the new world. Spider Grandmother took a net that she had knitted and carefully tied dewdrops on. With all her might, she threw that net into the heavens.

And on the first night of the new world, a million stars began to glow.

Aztlan

Mexica (Nahua) tradition

Cranes as white as purest salt,
clear water from the fountainhead,
blue skies above that peaceful isle:
how I long to return to Aztlan!

It was an island of resplendent whiteness, ringed by waters of turquoise blue, teeming with herons with snowy plumage. The sun rose above its horizon like a bird of fire. Emeralds rained when the poet prince sang his flower songs. The wise men of that realm recorded in books the path of the stars across the night sky with ink both red and black.

The people called it Aztlan, meaning Place of Whiteness, some say, or Isle of Herons, others claim. It seemed eternal, and perhaps it was. The golden sandals of the gods themselves trod those polished roads. Boats plied its placid waters, weighted with flowers and precious crops: golden corn and sweet pumpkins, cocoa used to make the sacred drink, and every possible hue of chili pepper.

Purest air and bluest sky. Warm and gentle weather, balanced from north to south, serene from east to west. A land of ruddy sunset splendor and deep green night, of dawn drowsing in the branches of the trees and the mockingbird's four hundred songs.

It seemed eternal and perhaps it was. Then the god Huitzilopochtli—Blue Hummingbird of the South, tireless guardian of the sun—appeared in majesty before Mexitli, a proud prince and pious priest, while he made sacrifices in the temple, pricking his thighs with maguey spines to offer up his own precious blood.

"Mexitli, my mirror," said Huitzilopochtli, "you must lead our people toward another destiny. There is no time to lose. Blow the sacred conch in all four directions; let its trumpeting voice be heard. The creators above have decreed the end of Aztlan, so you must paint yourselves a new beginning."

Confusion and fear swirled in Mexitli's heart, hearing the order of Huitzilopochtli. Would Aztlan disappear? Would the white island sink into the turquoise waters? He dared not ask, but that blue hummingbird could read the chieftain's mind. The god frowned.

"Aztlan will neither sink nor disappear, because it is eternal. But very soon, no one will be able to see it. It has fulfilled its purpose, the design for which the creators forged it. Now, Mexitli, my mirror, tell me: will you obey?"

The prince fell to his knees, pressing his forehead on the ground before the majesty of Huitzilopochtli. The god smiled, satisfied at what he saw within Mexitli's brave heart.

"You shall take the people on a long pilgrimage. They will walk to the South, and on the way, women will bear children that will inherit a new world. Now you see me clearly, but soon it will be impossible for you to distinguish the contours of my body. However, I will be with you all, accompanying my people on their lengthy trek. Sometimes you will see my footprints in the sand."

Finally, Mexitli managed to speak, without daring to look up at the face of his god.

"How will we know where to stop? How will we know where to establish that new world?"

"The signal will be very clear, Prince Mexitli, my mirror. Your tribe will arrive at a turquoise lake, the very eye of Chalchiuht-licue, goddess of the water skirt. On an isle in that lake stands a cactus upon which an eagle will perch, a serpent gripped in its claws. To many that place will seem inhospitable. Some will think it impossible to build a single house upon its rocky soil, let alone a temple. But look now with the eye of your mind: upon that barren stone your tribe will found Aztlan once more. In time the herons will arrive on their salt-white wings, and a city will rise, surrounded by glimmering light, like the feathers of a quetzal."

"What name shall we give that land?" the prince asked, intoxicated by this vision of the future.

"Yours, Mexitli, my mirror. Your place, your seat. Mexico: the foundation of heaven."

Bacabs

Maya tradition

Wardens of the sky:
four pillars,
four colors,
four Bacabs.

They never tire,
they never die.
They are the healers:
they keep the rites.

Before time began, there was Itzamna. He was the universe, and within him all things existed: white and black, good and bad, woman and man, stone and water. One day, Itzamna noticed a woman weaving the hems of the cosmos. She was beautiful to his eyes, so he called her to him. Her name was Ix Chebel Yax. She wore snakes as a headdress and loved color and beauty. With a soft brush, at the edge of space and time, she had painted red the clay she loved, the leaves of some trees, and the crest of the woodpecker.

In those distant days, the thirteen levels of heaven creaked and groaned, threatening to collapse upon the heads of all living beings.

Itzamna and Ix Chebel Yax, universe and weaver, husband and wife, looked each other in the eyes, worried. He said:

"My wife, as creators, our duty is to endow the world with what it lacks."

"You speak of the weight of the heavens?" she asked.

"Indeed. I had a dream, perhaps a vision, in which I saw the sky fall upon the earth. We must provide the heavens with supports. I thought about the trees, but none grows high enough to reach from its roots to the clouds."

"Leave it to me," said Ix Chebel Yax. "I am a diligent weaver. Besides, I am your wife."

As she left to craft a solution, Itzamna crossed his arms and bowed his head, seeking to rest at the edge of a cenote. At that moment, a piece of heaven fell at his feet, disturbing his peace.

A few days later, Ix Chebel Yax informed her resplendent husband that they now had four sons. She had borne them all at one time: that was how things were done during the age of the gods.

"They are called Bacabs," said Ix Chebel Yax to Itzamna, "each one a different color. They are the product of my hard work and of your concern for the welfare of all living things. They are already prepared to shoulder the weight of heaven. They will stand forever at the four corners of the world, keeping the vault of the sky aloft. The red Bacab, Kantziknal, will guard the East; the white one, Saksini, the North; the yellow one, Hobnil, the South; and the black one, Hosanek, the West."

Itzamna gave each of the Bacabs a huge ceiba tree to lean upon should they feel fatigue. But it was not necessary, since they had inherited the diligence of their weaver mother. They never tired—though their muscles were tense and their eyes fixed, unblinking—of fulfilling their task of holding up the sky.

At first, the Bacabs were visible to human beings, since women and men were dedicated to understanding the world and always in need of cures for their hunger and thirst, their worries and their illnesses. People of those early ages asked the Bacabs for advice, and the gods answered willingly, without ceasing to support the sky. They smiled sweetly when they revealed what plant or root could treat some disease.

Over the centuries, the Bacabs became covered with foliage and earth, with clouds and dust storms, until their beautiful faces were no longer visible. However, their teachings became rituals, and their words of healing and consolation were engraved in stone using the beautiful glyphs invented by their father, Itzamna, who also was the universe.

Bochica

Muisca tradition

With your crook,
wise Bochica,
with your staff,
you fly to the East.

Just promise that you
will return to stand
here in Colombia
as now we call your land.

From the East came a foreigner to the lands of Bacatá, which we know as Bogotá. He was different in every way from the Muisca people, who did not know in those distant times how to cultivate the earth, weave fabric or shape clay. They lived as best they could day by day, struggling to survive. They hunted animals with stones and ate the meat raw. With untanned hides they covered themselves. They spoke—if it one could call that speech—with grunts and signs. Their nails were dirty and very few grew to be old, because disease took many lives. They lived in caves and their nights were very dark, spent without light and without words.

Until Bochica arrived. His hair was the color of silver, his eyes as blue as the cloudless sky. He wore a long tunic knotted over his left shoulder, carried a sturdy walking stick and looked with infinite compassion at every person he encountered. He was accompanied by an alpaca who died exhausted upon arriving at the town of Bosa.

There Bochica taught the people to speak, to cultivate, to weave and to sing. To build houses for shelter, to cook their food and to dream. When he left, he passed through Pasca and Fontibón, through Zipacón and Tunja, and wherever he visited, he left a legacy of beauty and truth.

Those who had become his followers noticed that every day there was more sadness in Bochica's eyes, as if he knew that soon he would have to leave the beautiful lands he had come to love, as if he sensed that his teachings would be forgotten. His steps led him back toward the East from which he had emerged, until he arrived at the town of Iza, in the Boyacá region. There he disappeared, merging with the light or the wind. No one knew what became of him.

Time passed: twenty years or two hundred or perhaps even two thousand. The Muisca set aside the teachings of Bochica and offended the gods, especially Chibchachum, protector of the Muisca lands and guardian of the waters. Their misuse of rivers and earth dirtied his face, attacking and disrespecting him until he lost his patience.

Chibchachum in his anger poured out the power of his waters, diverting rivers till they covered the savannah of Bacatá. Many drowned, humans and animals alike, until despair seized the remaining Muisca. Then the best among them remembered Bochica.

"He is human too! He will save us!"

"Come back, Bochica, our father, and save us from the wrath of Chibchachum!"

"Forgive us for forgetting your great teachings. Rescue us, Bochica. This time we will not let you down."

With even greater force and hatred the waters of Chibcha-chum roared when they heard these cries. His rage unleashed, the god focused his devastating power, hoping to destroy humanity completely.

But Bochica heard the voices of despair from his mysterious abode. He returned, his silver hair and blue eyes unaltered by time. Resplendent, Bochica summoned the caciques of the Muisca people to accompany him to the Tequendama region. The people followed their rulers in silence, wringing their hands and looking toward the sky.

Suddenly, a rainbow formed, and to the amazement of the Muisca, Bochica trod upward along the seven colors as if they were a bridge. He stopped before the rocks of a high promontory and struck them with his walking stick. All the waters of Chibchachum that had caused the flood of the savannah rushed to gather in that place, forming a massive cascade. The Muisca named it Tequendama, It Comes Rushing Down.

His heart free of resentment or doubt, Bochica decided that justice should be restored. Chibchachum had acted excessively even for an offended god. Bochica decreed that as punishment, the deity must now carry the earth on his back. So he has done ever since, and when an earthquake trembles underfoot, it is because the tired god is shrugging his shoulders to shift the weight of the world.

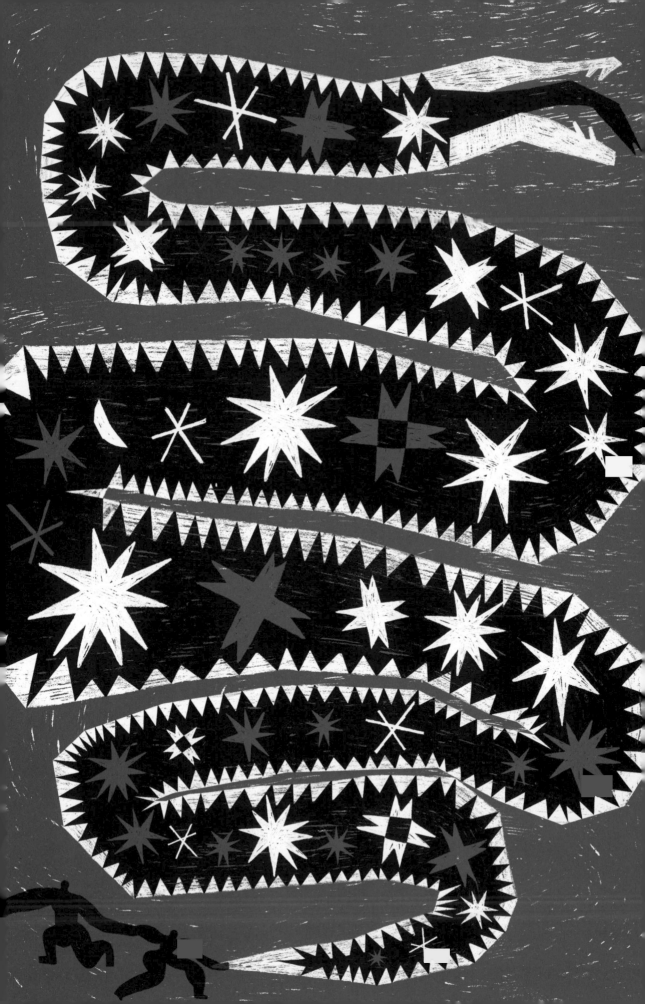

Coatlicue

Mexica (Nahua) tradition

Coatlicue sweeps
the mountaintop.
The goddess trembles,
as the full moon drops.

The stars begin
to shimmer bright.
But Huitzilopochtli
will soon arrive.

Upon Mount Coatepec, hill of serpents, stood a temple of red walls with beautiful frescoes. In an interior patio, whose walls were topped with crenels to follow the passage of the stars, a beautiful goddess slowly swept the stucco floor. Her name was Coatlicue, mother of the wandering and innumerable stars, the Centzonhuitznahuah, and of the valiant moon, the goddess with bells on her cheeks, Coyolxauhqui.

Coatlicue swept serenely, the whisper of the broom the only sound. The serpents painted on her skirt seemed to undulate with every rhythmic movement.

Suddenly, from the heights of heaven or perhaps from deep within it—only the gods knew for certain—a blue feather fell. It floated down gently, as if lying back in the air. Coatlicue paused in her task and watched, fascinated by the feather's lightness, drawn to its color. Finally, the feather landed on the ground. The goddess could not resist the temptation to pick it up. Impulsively, she tucked it into her waistband, between her skin and her skirt. And she kept on sweeping.

When she went to rest in her room, she looked for the blue feather, thinking to keep it in a box of carved wood, but it was gone. She sighed in resignation. Still, she swore she would always keep alive in her memory the unearthly blue and lightness of the vision she had enjoyed in the courtyard of the temple.

The following days Coatlicue felt the desire to sing and take flight. But she belonged to the earth, so she could not. A few days later, she realized she was pregnant. The news brought her joy.

"Now that I have borne the moon and the stars," she told herself, "this new birth will be even more magnificent. I will have a son in whom is concentrated all the intense blue of the universe, the lightness of the air, the brilliance of the light."

Days became weeks, then months. One afternoon, Coyolxauhqui peered out the window to watch her mother. With silver eyes, she saw that Coatlicue's figure had widened. The moon goddess realized her mother was expecting a son.

The one with bells on her cheeks was furious. Only she and her brothers, the Centzonhuitznahuah—Four Hundred Southern Stars—should exist.

"How could you dare?" roared Coyolxauhqui in the deep night sky.

Coatlicue raised her head. She saw her daughter in full regalia, guardian of the heavens, shaking her warrior shield. She feared for her coming son, so she sent a prayer winging its way inward, to her own womb, where that child of blue light, her beloved son, was growing larger.

In a frenzied rage, Coyolxauhqui hurtled through the fields of heaven upon her silver sandals. She found her brothers, the Four Hundred Southern Stars, practicing launching spears from their atlatls.

"To me, Centzonhuitznahuah! Our mother has betrayed us! She will soon give birth to a son who will attempt to destroy us. We must avoid that birth at all costs and annihilate Coatlicue before our doom emerges from her womb."

The Southern Stars burned with hunger for war and spread their luminous bodies on a journey through the night sky to Mount Coatepec. Coatlicue had taken refuge in the temple. From the same courtyard where she had picked up the blue feather, she saw the misfortune that was looming over her.

"Help me, my son!" she cried. "Do not let your siblings annihilate me and thus prevent your birth."

From within the warmth of her womb or perhaps from the depths of heaven—only the creators knew for certain—came the voice of her bright blue child.

"Do not worry, Mother. I will protect you. Now watch in amazement what happens next."

At the precise moment when the furious moon loomed above the head of Coatlicue, followed by her four hundred brothers, the goddess who had once swept the stucco of the temple gave birth to the invincible Hummingbird of the South: Huitzilopochtli. Armed with his fiery serpent, Xiuhcoatl, he confronted his powerful siblings. The sky of that cosmic night burst into flame as the stellar children of Coatlicue began to clash. First fell the Southern Stars: one by one they were destroyed.

Then it was Coyolxauhqui's turn. Her end had come. The beautiful warrior gave a thundering cry when her powerful brother grabbed her by the hair and mercilessly severed her head. Down the rocky slopes of Mount Coatepec, Huitzilopochtli hurled the moon, which shattered in pieces at the foot of the hill.

From the courtyard of the temple, daylight flooded the world.

And a tiny hummingbird spread its wings, hovering for a few seconds over Coatlicue's head.

Hummingbird

Guarani tradition

This is the story
of Fleet and Flower,
both drawn together
by love's immense power.

The world pulled them apart,
their hopes it devoured.
Let us hope that one day
Fleet finds his Flower!

In the enchanted land that spreads fragrant under the gaze of Tupa, father god and creator, there once lived long ago a maiden named Poty: Flower. She was the daughter of the cacique of her tribe, adorned with every beauty in the world. Her voice was sweet as the wind blowing through the reeds of the river, and her black tresses cascaded over her shoulders like a cape. Flower wove delicate white blossoms into her hair, and when she walked, she seemed to be carrying the starry night sky. In her eyes a mysterious light glowed every time she daydreamed, for Flower liked to imagine that one day she would visit the abode of the moon god, whom her Guarani people named Jasy.

Flower enjoyed ambling along the river in a forest near her tribal lands. During one of those walks, the moon god peered at her from the sky and felt so much sympathy for the young woman that, without her asking, he decided to grant her a wish.

"What do humans want most?" Jasy asked himself from his silver balcony.

"Love," he replied to himself. Inspired, he sent his son—the golden Jasy Jatere, fragment of the moon—in the shape of a bird to whisper a sweet melody in Flower's ear.

Flower heard an unfamiliar song. Fascinated, she stopped her walk, listening. At that moment, a young nobleman, son of the cacique of the neighboring tribe, came running along with a lightness that caught the attention of the maid.

Mainumby, the young man was called. Fleet. When he caught sight of Flower, he slowed to a stop. He had already heard of the beautiful daughter of the cacique of the other tribe, princess of the people who had sworn eternal war against his own.

Fleet had never seen a woman more beautiful than Flower.

Flower thought Fleet the most gorgeous man she had ever laid eyes upon.

The two stood there, staring at each other, while on a nearby branch, a bird kept on singing—the yellow-feathered Jasy Jatere, fulfilling the command of his father, the moon.

On that day, their fingers entwined, Fleet and Flower promised to love each other forever. They would meet on the riverbank, lying to their respective families, knowing that, because their people were enemies, their love was forbidden.

But the feelings in their hearts were so intense and present that they did not think about the future. Instead, they were content to see each other for a few minutes each day before separating, promising to return. The river flowed along, babbling silver verses. The branches of the trees swayed in time. Glints of gold poured from the heavens. Fleet and Flower were happy, and Jasy smiled from his silver balcony as he watched their love grow.

One day when the sky dawned covered with clouds, blocking out the sun and threatening a storm, the cacique sent for his daughter. Flower arrived in her father's presence, her heart aching with unease.

"The time has come for you to take a husband. Within a month, you will marry Mbarete, the bravest and strongest young man of our tribe."

Flower bit her lip to keep from screaming. She could not oppose her father's will. If she mentioned Fleet, she would provoke his anger and perhaps cause the death of her beloved. Those were difficult times, when strife between the rival tribes grew dry and brittle like a drought-stricken forest. Any provocation could reignite it.

The young woman walked for the last time to meet the man she loved on the riverbank. But that day Fleet did not arrive. His father had entrusted him to head an expedition to hunt a dangerous jaguar, which had been terrorizing the members of his tribe.

Desperate, Flower knelt under a large tree and asked the god Tupa to save her from that wedding, to protect the life of her beloved Fleet:

"Father Tupa, I beg you, do with me as you like, but save me from a wedding I do not want. Transform me, hide me, save me, Tupa."

The creator took pity on her. Wise beyond all human understanding, he chose to turn the maiden into a flower and take her to a place known only to him, deep in the Guarani jungle.

The wind shook the leaves of the tree under which Flower had knelt, rushing off to tell the moon what had transpired.

After seven days, Fleet returned to his village, greeted by the drums of his tribe, victorious in his fight against the jaguar, whose spotted carcass hung from a pole, carried by two of the bravest warriors. Once the celebrations concluded, the warrior hurried to the riverbank to meet with Flower.

She never came.

Fleet returned day after day, to no avail. At the end of the ninth, he conceived a desperate plan: he would seek her out among the enemy tribe, knowing that he risked his very life. But Jasy, moved by the young man's sadness, came down from heaven in human form and told Fleet what had happened.

"I will look for my precious Flower wherever she is!" the young man exclaimed with vehemence.

"Only Tupa knows where she is," Jasy said.

"Do you, by chance, know what sort of flower he has turned her into?" Fleet asked.

"Only Tupa knows," Jasy repeated, transforming into a beam of silver light and returning to heaven.

Fleet then knelt under the same tree as Flower had and prayed with all the strength of his heart to the creator:

"Father Tupa, I beg you, do with me as you like, but help me find my Flower. Transform me, force me, command me, Tupa."

The creator turned the light-footed Fleet into a hummingbird. And since then, without ever tiring, he roams the Guarani jungle, flitting from flower to flower, searching for his beloved.

Great Flood

Andean tradition

Water above, water below:
the flood begins to flow.
With vicuñas, alpacas,
with jaguars and llamas,

with a soaking wet fox,
roosters, and macaws,
a shepherd climbs a hill
until the flood at last is still.

In the Tahuantinsuyo—the four quadrants into which the Incas divided the world, the proud city of Cuzco at its center—there was once a shepherd whose only company was a llama that he loved very much. On one occasion, returning from the market or catu, the man realized that his llama was hungry.

He soon found a spot carpeted with the best grass, seemingly ideal for feeding his llama. As always, the shepherd tied her to a tree so that the animal would concentrate on devouring the surrounding grass. To his surprise, the llama did not eat a bite. Instead, she just stared at him with eyes so sad they made the man want to cry.

"Dear little llama, why won't you eat?"

"Yu yu," the llama whispered, tugging at the rope around her neck.

"Did I offend you in some way? Haven't I treated you well? Did I perhaps put too heavy a load upon your back?" asked the shepherd, who liked to speak with his llama because she always listened to him. As is the case for any animal, however, she could not answer him. She lacked the gift of speech.

"Yu yu," the llama insisted, bringing her snout closer to the mouth of the man, who was chewing on choclo, a tender ear of large-kernel corn he had been saving to eat until his llama was grazing. With a quick movement, she knocked the corn to the ground. The shepherd was furious. Muttering a curse, the man scolded his animal.

"Foolish llama! Ungrateful beast! Why do you complain so much? Don't you see that I have brought you to the best pastures of the Tahuantinsuyo?"

The llama spat into the man's face, something she had never done during their whole life together, and said:

"*You* are the fool! You have *no* idea what's about to happen!"

"What? You can talk!" The man was amazed, wiping the llama's sticky saliva from his face.

"Of course I can. I haven't before because it wasn't necessary," the llama replied. "I'll tell you the cause of my sadness, the reason I didn't even want to taste the delicious grass. While you were bartering in the catu, I talked—in my people's way, of course—with an old llama. She revealed to me what is going to happen, starting today."

"And what's going to happen?" asked the alarmed man. "Speak, dear little llama. Tell me everything you know."

The llama sighed. Lowering her voice almost to a whisper, she said, "For five days, from the clouds will fall so much rain that the sea will rise. It won't stop rising until it floods the entire earth.

All creatures that live, move, feed and breathe upon the face of the world will drown. To be clear: everything is going to die."

The shepherd thought he might faint. Death was near and his llama knew it! He went on to say, with a voice as thin as the streams at the bottom of the imposing canyons of the Tahuantin-suyo, "Is there anything we can do to save ourselves?"

"The old llama told me to spread the word. We have to climb to the top of Mount Huillcacoto, carrying enough food and water to last five days."

The man gathered supplies and headed with his llama toward Mount Huillcacoto. It was a difficult ascent, but the two companions pushed on, spurred by their desire not to drown to death. All living beings want to continue living. It is a desire shared by men and llamas alike.

When he reached the top, the man opened his eyes wide. There was hardly any room to stand on that summit because of how many llamas, alpacas, vicuñas and guanacos were gathered there, as well as wildcats of all sizes, boars, snakes and crocodiles. There were so many birds perched in the trees that crowned the top of Mount Huillcacoto the branches groaned, threatening to break. Macaws, owls, seagulls and hundreds of thousands of tunkis, cocks of the rock, made such a raucous noise that the man could no longer hear his llama. But she had already said what she needed to say.

Lightning flashed, thunder rumbled and a torrential downpour began to fall. From the top of the mountain, the shepherd saw the waters begin to flood the world. They rose inexorably and covered everything, threatening to devour Mount Huillcacoto itself. The waters of the sea, reinforced by the waters of the sky, began to spill onto the summit. The space for the shepherd and the assembled animals began to shrink, so they squeezed together as much as they could. Not a single crocodile thought of devouring even the smallest alpaca, nor did a single owl consider hunting some sparrow. There was a fox that couldn't keep itself completely on dry land: the tip of its tail spent the five days of the flood submerged in the sea.

The rain finally ended, the waters began to recede gradually and the sea level returned to normal. The animals descended from the mountain in a joyful throng and the birds launched themselves into the sky.

"And the fox?" the shepherd asked.

"Because the tip of his tail was submerged so long in sea water, it changed color: it's now black," the llama answered as she chewed vigorously on a succulent tuft of grass the color of the emerald.

The shepherd lived the rest of his life alone but grateful to his llama, for having saved him from the flood that wiped out every other human being that had once lived in the Tahuantinsuyo.

Golden King

Muisca tradition

A man of gold
stands on a raft:
through Lake Guatavita
he guides his craft.

Emeralds fall,
the birds now sing.
He's El Dorado:
it's life he brings.

The king or zipa of Guatavita was very powerful. He reigned over prosperous lands, owned splendid houses, commanded brave warriors. No one was permitted to look him in the face. His word was the law. He had many wives, as was the custom in those days, because he needed a psihipqua, an heir, a son who would succeed him when the time came.

Among his many wives, he loved none as much as sweet Moon, a princess with almond eyes and lips as soft as flower petals. She bore him a child in whose features the king of Guatavita saw himself reflected. He was sure that, of all his children, that prince would be his successor.

Perhaps the gods, or fate, or that dark force that is determined to overwhelm the light decided that the beautiful Moon would fall in love with one of the captains of the Muisca army, and that he would be willing to give his life for her, so deeply did he fall in love with his king's wife. Though they tried to keep their love hidden, the powerful zipa received the shocking news, what he

considered the greatest misfortune ever to befall him. He condemned the captain to a horrible death before Moon's eyes.

She became sick with sadness. One night she took her son in her arms and went silently to Lake Guatavita. She dropped like a stone, clutching her son as they sank. The lake drew them down into its unfathomable depths, and there mother and son became ghostly inhabitants of the waters.

When the king of Guatavita learned what had happened, he felt his heart might explode. He sent one of his wizards to the lake, demanded that he dive deep and recover his wife and son.

"Alive! I want them back alive!" he roared with madness and pain.

The wizard asked to be left alone and closed his eyes. He focused heart, soul and mind, traveling to the depths of Lake Guatavita without getting wet or risking his life. There he saw the beautiful Moon sitting on a throne of emeralds. In her lap sat the little prince, smiling and playing with a gold disc his mother had tied around his neck. The lady smiled at the wizard with great sweetness and extended her open hand, palm upward. In it was a polished emerald.

The wizard understood the message and thus passed it along to the bereaved king of Guatavita. "Your wife and your son are now gods beneath the waters. As such they ask you to institute a ritual: offerings of gold and emeralds, consecrated to their spirits, from today until forever."

The wizard fell silent out of respect. The face of his king so twisted with the greatness of his pain that the wizard hesitated to tell him the full message he had received. But there was no other choice. The messages of the gods cannot be betrayed.

"There is something else."

"What is it?" the king asked, his voice cracking with grief.

"You must offer yourself."

After a night of meditation contemplating the bright moon, the zipa knew what he had to do. He called together his counselors and explained to them the ritual that from that day forward would be repeated each time a new prince rose to the throne of Guatavita.

A large crowd gathered around the lake, men and women adorned with flowers and multicolored feathers. They all cast sad looks at the water, knowing that within its heart dwelled the spirits of Moon and her son. At about midday, surrounded by his principal nobles, the great zipa of Guatavita made his appearance. He stripped off his robes, set aside his mantle and the nobles began to smear a sticky resin over his body. Then they sprinkled his body with fine gold dust obtained from a vessel decorated with circles and triangles. To the people on the shore, their king seemed a man made of gold. Shimmering in the rays of the sun, he boarded a raft loaded with offerings of gold and emeralds for the spirits of the lake.

The raft sailed the calm waters. When it reached the center, the zipa began to throw the precious objects overboard, one by one. A gentle breeze swept along the surface of the lake, stirring the feathers and clothes of the people. They had watched the offerings be delivered. Now they knew those gifts had been received.

It was only then that the zipa raised his arms to the sky, like a resplendent human bird, and plunged into the sacred waters of the Guatavita lagoon.

Such was the end of the golden king. El Dorado, the Spanish would one day mutter in greedy amazement. But his realm is peopled by ghosts now, there in the watery depths. The living can never reach it.

Brave Souls of
the Dead

Mapuche tradition

Four wise whales
that lead to infinity.

That wonderful island
where we become spirit.

That day, Am was surprised to find herself in the middle of a group of people whose faces were familiar to her. The night before, she had fallen asleep, shivering with fever. She remembered her dream: she had been crossing a place in the forest that she had frequented as a child. She could recognize her favorite tree. The light of the moon, filtered through those branches, caressed her skin and cooled her fever.

But now Am was surrounded by people she had known before. She recognized her aunt Amaru and her cousin Nahuel. She wanted to approach them, but to her surprise and without warning, everyone began to scream and beat the ground with hands and feet.

"Run, Am! Run for your life! Escape before the wekufe catches you, before the calcu enslave you!"

The wekufe! The calcu! Am shuddered. The people were screaming, but they were looking off in every direction, as if they could not see her, as if Am was invisible. The wekufe and the

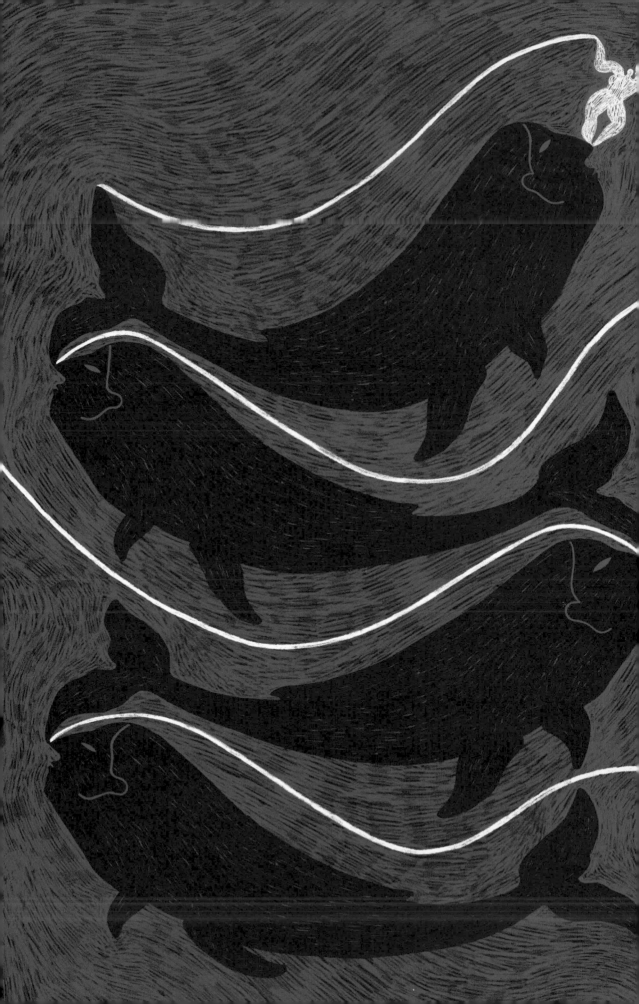

calcu—that demon and its sorcerers, featured in stories that had frightened her as a child—were apparently real, perhaps hiding behind her relatives or under the roots of the trees.

She had to flee. Am started running like mad, so fast she felt her legs had sprouted wings. The voice of her aunt Amaru called faintly after her, "Remember, Am! You have to get to the island of Ngill Chenmaywe. Only the wise Trempulkalwe can help you!"

Am went on running. Out of curiosity, she turned her head to see if the calcu and the wekufe were following her. A huge black swirling mass rushed after her, closer and closer. Terrified, Am pushed herself harder, faster, until her feet hardly touched the ground. She crossed woods and mountains, lighter with every passing second, nearly free from the darkness that pursued her. She felt brave and bold, a bird wheeling its way across the heavens.

At last she reached the sea. Its glittering surface blinded her.

Am stopped on the shore. Full of joy, she let the waves lap at her bare feet. How beautiful the world was! How free she felt, standing before such an immense expanse of blue! She pressed her hands together and closed her eyes in prayer. When she opened them again, there were four old women with kind faces standing in the shallows, each dressed in a different color.

"You took a long time, my daughter," said the old woman in blue.

"We were getting worried," added the old woman in black.

"Your grandparents told us you would come," said the old woman in green.

"And you are just in time! The sun is beginning to set," said the old woman in red.

Sure enough, the huge golden disc of the sun was sinking into the sea.

Am could not contain her tears at the unsurpassed beauty of that moment. She wanted to answer the old women, but suddenly they were gone.

"Follow us!" shouted a powerful voice from the sea.

Four whales of different colors drifted upon the waves, waiting for Am. She knew at once that these were the wise Trempulkalwe, which her aunt Amaru had mentioned at the beginning of her desperate flight.

Am wiped away her tears. Just as she had run and nearly flown before, she now dove into the ocean, swimming briskly to follow the whales. The sun set, but they traveled all night. With each stroke, Am became stronger. Soon she had completely forgotten the squirming black mass. She just focused on swimming.

At dawn a glittering island appeared before her eyes.

"We have arrived," said the blue whale.

"It's the island of Ngill Chenmaywe," the black whale announced.

"Where the brave dead arrive," explained the green whale.

"Here you will transform into pure spirit. Then you will be able to return to your loved ones," the red whale whispered.

"Forever," said Am, setting her foot on the blessed island, which Chileans call Mocha Island, where the brave souls of the dead go to rejoin the universal spirit, Pu-Am, which is in everything, in the water and in the name, in the trees and in the sky. Reunited with the whole, they will live forever in the beautiful and free Mapuche land.

Bunched Stars

Niitsitapi (Blackfoot) tradition

Six children of earth
have now become stars.
When they want, they send rain;
if they want, they send drought.
"Moon, moon," howls the wolf.
The dog cries, "Moon, moon."
The earth is so dry—
please send us the rain!

In the northernmost extremes of the world, that land of purest skies and infinite lakes bordered by dunes, there once lived a family with six sons. Theirs was the poorest family in the camp. The father was not a good hunter, and the mother only managed to gather a handful of roots and berries each day. They mostly survived on the charity of others.

Each spring, when the skin of the baby buffalo takes on a beautiful reddish hue, the men prepared to hunt them so their wives could make garments of that color for their children. But this father was too poor and unskilled to participate in these great hunts.

As a result, the six brothers never had red robes. Over time, children their age began to tease them, laughing at their misery. Even adults murmured behind their parents' backs about the family's dwindling resources.

One day, the eldest of the brothers gathered the other five and said, "If next spring we do not receive red robes, if we find ourselves once more wearing still-brown clothes made from the skin of old buffalo, we'll leave the camp and live in the sky."

"But how? We don't have wings!" said the youngest.

"We'll find a way," the eldest replied. He had been observing the rituals of the camp's aged sage and had already sketched out a plan.

The next spring, after the great hunt concluded, the six brothers found themselves again without red robes. They met in a clearing in the forest and sat in a circle. The eldest spoke:

"Today is the day for keeping our promise. Today is the day we head for the sky because we don't have red robes."

The fourth of the brothers said, "I wish we could take the water with us, all of it—from the camp and the surrounding land—to punish those who were cruel to us and made fun of our parents for being poor."

The second brother added, "We should take our three dogs with us. They aren't guilty of anything and shouldn't go thirsty."

Then, the eldest brother took weasel hair that he had prepared and put some strands on the backs of his brothers and their dogs. He took another bunch of hair and put it in his mouth. With the rest he rubbed his hands and said—just as he had seen the aged sage do:

"Now, close your eyes."

This is what the brothers did, making sure their dogs also

closed their own. The eldest brother blew the weasel hairs in his mouth toward the sky.

When the brothers opened their eyes, they found themselves in the lodge of the Sun and the Moon. All six fell to their knees. An old man with long white hair and a dazzling glare was the Sun. A beautiful young woman with hair as black as night was the Moon. Both husband and wife were surprised to see six children from the earth kneeling at their feet.

The Moon said in a sweet and melodious voice, "Children of the earth, why have you come to our house in the sky?"

The third brother replied, "We never got red robes in spring, so people made fun of us. We have come to ask for your help."

"And what can we do?" asked the Moon.

The fourth brother, whose idea it had been, said, "We wish that for seven days there be no water on earth, not a drop in the rivers or in the ravines."

The Sun frowned. It was asking too much.

"Are you not going to help these children who managed against all odds to ascend to the sky?" demanded the Moon.

The Sun was silent, but the Moon insisted, "We will help you, boys, but in exchange for what you ask, you must remain in the heavens forever."

The brothers nodded. The Sun at last agreed to the Moon's terms.

How dry, how hot the next day on earth was! So much so, the water of rivers and lakes boiled and then evaporated. And the night! A torture for the inhabitants of the earth, who could not fall asleep, throats dry, mouths parched.

Then some took their dogs to the dry riverbed. The animals dug holes so deep they spouted weak springs that soon dried up as well. The rays of the Sun were so hot men had to take refuge in them.

The seventh night, the leader of the dogs—an old white hound that had lived with wolves in his youth—began to howl pitifully to the Moon. He apologized to those boys who never had red robes and begged compassion for his withering land.

The next day, a benevolent rain cooled the earth. Life returned, the plants grew, the buffalo came back to graze in the meadows, and the lakes—the Great Lakes—they once more became the Moon's favorite place to gaze.

The brothers and their dogs stayed forever in the sky, where they can still be seen. Their people call them Miohpoisiks, the Bunched Stars. Others know them as the Pleiades. When they disappear in the evening, the people of the North know that the rains will soon fall and all thirst will be quenched.

Sak Nikte

Maya tradition

Bloom of the moon,
you whitest of flowers:
never stop hoping,
for he will come soon.

Though the journey be sad,
together in love,
you will guide your people,
flower of the Mayab.

How beautiful was the princess Sak Nikte, white flower of the Mayab! She had just turned fifteen and stood looking at the sky, sighing, leaning on the balustrade of a balcony in the palace of her father, the powerful king of Mayapan.

Down one of the walkways came Prince Kanek, heir to the throne of Chichen Itza, the white city of the Itza people.

Sak Nikte felt her heart slip away like a trembling dove. The sight of Prince Kanek left her giddy with love in a single instant. When the warrior raised his eyes and saw the princess, a sigh rose in his chest. He committed that vision to heart, so that he could better remember her when he returned to his kingdom, falling on his knees before the memory of those black eyes, that hair in its beautiful and complicated braid, the jade bracelets and gold earrings that adorned the princess.

Talk to her? Impossible. Kanek knew too well that the princess was betrothed to Ulil, the heir to the kingdom of Uxmal. The marriage had been arranged since her birth and her destiny read in the book of days. That agreement could not be broken, because in it rested the pure and continued strength of the League, which had led to prosperity in the cities of Chichen Itza, Uxmal and Mayapan.

"Destiny is wrong. The book must have been misread!" cried Princess Sak Nikte in her room on the eve of her wedding. "I do not want to marry Ulil! I do not want to go to Uxmal! I love Kanek and want to live in the city of the Itza."

Sak Nikte cried throughout the night, her long hair reflecting the moonlight. And the goddess of the moon, Ixchel, sighed at the pain of her most beloved daughter. She turned her beautiful face to light the fragrant night of Chichen Itza and to learn Kanek's true feelings.

The prince could not sleep. He wandered the open corridors of his mansion. He had been invited to the wedding, which would take place in Uxmal. He could not refuse. The Mayapan League came first. But his brain burned, his hands trembled, his soul flitted back to the memory of his precious white flower.

Suddenly, a noise caught his attention. Thinking it was an animal, he put himself on guard.

"Kanek, what are you waiting for?"

It was the voice of an old man, creaky and slightly mocking.

A figure stepped into the moonlight. The prince was startled to see that it was an alux, one of the magical Little Folk. For a moment, he felt he was dreaming. Words failed him.

Into the silence, the old elf spoke again:

"That white flower rests in the grass, waiting for you. Will you let someone else cut it?"

Kanek wanted to roar "no" like a jaguar, to demand how the alux could know his feelings if he had not said a word to anyone. But before his eyes the old elf vanished, becoming darkness and night, leaving a poisonous stain on the soul of the prince.

The day of the wedding arrived. Sak Nikte emerged from her chambers, pallid. She had cried all night and could not take the heartache anymore. Two master stoneworkers presented the king of Uxmal a stele upon which the names of Sak Nikte and Ulil had been engraved. The bride shuddered, knowing there was no escape. The moment her name was set in stone, she was tied to the long count of the years alongside Ulil. The artists read with trembling voices the text they had carved in the stele:

"From them will come the greatness of the Mayab. From them will come peace and abundance, our past and our future."

Sak Nikte burst into tears. Everyone thought she had been moved by the greatness of her destiny.

The guests of the neighboring cities began to arrive, the nobles of Copan, the princes of Yaxchilan. Offerings from Kibilba were paraded about . . . but the most awaited, the most important ally, Prince Kanek, was slow to appear.

The time came to hold the ceremony. Copal incense burned in the censers. The priests sang the sacred hymns. But when Ulil gave his bride the cocoa beans that the holy rite requires, the wedding song was drowned out by war cries.

The elegant guests stirred, the feathers of their headdresses trembling. Kanek, with sixty of his warriors, burst into the ceremony and took Sak Nikte in his arms. The raid was so quick that no one made the slightest attempt to prevent it. As quickly and surprisingly as they had arrived, the Itza fighters left Uxmal.

But after three days the angry lords of Mayapan and Uxmal had raised their powerful armies. They marched against Chichen

Itza, determined to inflict cruel death on Kanek and recover Sak Nikte.

When they arrived, howling their own terrifying war cries, they found the city abandoned. Not a single inhabitant remained among its white stones. Confused at first, they soon understood that Kanek had fled with his people and the princess in order to escape the League's revenge. Roaring with frustrated fury, the warriors berserked against the beautiful city, smashing their maces against its sculptures, sundering its lintels, burning its buildings and erasing the path of the Feathered Serpent.

Where did the Itza people go? No one in the Mayab heard another word about them, but they carried love and sought peace. Although they had lost everything, they walked wandering under the stars, trusting their two guides: Prince Kanek and Princess Sak Nikte, the white flower of the Mayab.

Land of Fire

Selk'nam (Ona) tradition

Land of ice,	you are legend:
of peace and dreams,	we call you Fire.

Behind the stars in the East dwells Temaukel, a being of formless energy and vital word. He created everything and populated the earth, filling it with guanacos and swans, cypresses and cinnamon trees. To rule them, he made the Howenh: lesser gods and goddesses who adorned their bodies with mysterious images.

Among the Howenh, Moon stood out for her strength and dominion. She had gathered the goddesses Tempest, Sea, and Mountain to her side, filling them with power and convincing them that they were superior to the male gods. These—Sun, Wind, Rain, and Snow—lived in fear of their wives' power, for the goddesses had commanded them to hunt without ceasing in order to feed the terrible Xalpen: a monster, half rock and half flesh, who lived underground and wielded a razor-sharp nail on its index finger.

The monster had to be fed every hain, a ceremony celebrated when the young goddesses reached divine adulthood.

"If for the next hain, in three days, you have not brought twenty guanacos," Moon declared, "Xalpen will demand food, and she will start with you, Sun, even if you are my husband."

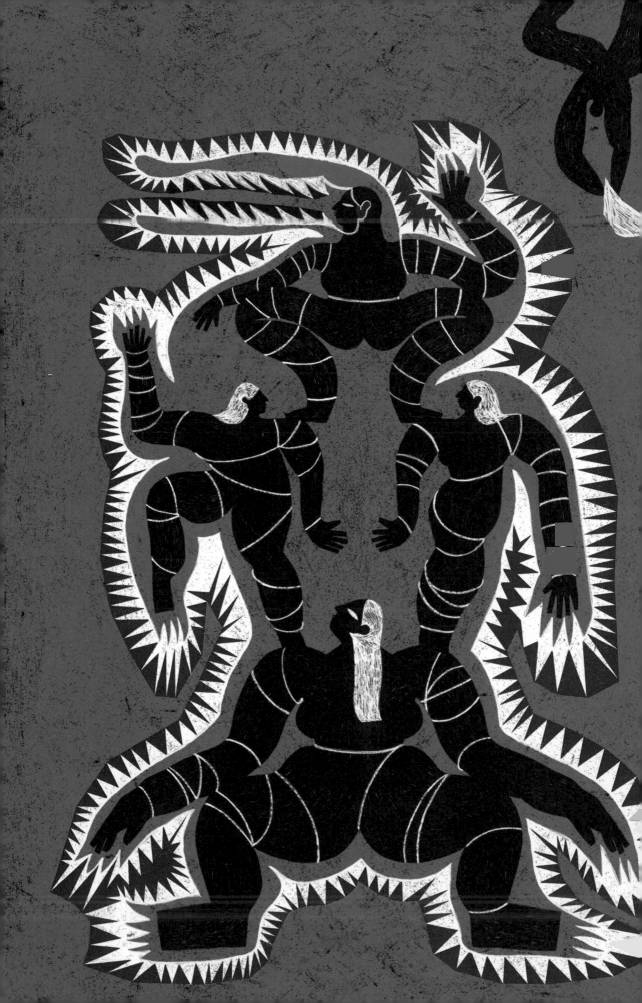

"Think, Wind," said the goddess Tempest to her husband, "how terrible it would be if Xalpen, with its sharp fingernail, instead of ripping through dead guanaco meat, sliced into one of you while you were still alive."

"Of course, you know, Rain, dearest husband," said the goddess Sea, "that you and the other gods must bring the fruits of your hunt, but never look to see what is happening inside the ceremonial hut."

"If you were to do so, Snow," said the goddess Mountain, "Xalpen would burst from the earth to devour you. Not one of you would be left alive!"

Fearful, the male gods made their way to the forest. They walked with heavy hearts, because they knew that it was impossible to get as many guanacos as their wives demanded.

However, Sun was lucky the first day and killed a robust adult that was wandering alone. As it fell beneath his arrows, Sun became sad. Such a beautiful animal, and he had been forced to end its life to appease a dark, underground monster the gods had never seen. But Sun had heard Xalpen roar and hit the earth, which had filled him with dread.

Throughout the rest of that day and the next, the hunters had no further luck. Sun decided to hurry home to give the goddesses the one guanaco he had felled and to ask for more time to comply with their request.

Overwhelmed by the weight of the dead animal, he came panting to the camp, only to find it empty. The goddesses were gathered in the ceremonial hut, a conical construction, formed by several trunks leaning against one another and covered with sewn guanaco skins.

Sun approached the hut and heard laughter, which surprised him a little. He left the dead guanaco on the ground and peered in through a gap that had formed when a strip of badly sewn skin fell off.

And what he saw! What he heard! The goddesses were sitting and joking, while building a structure of branches and covering it with skins.

"If the gods only knew that Xalpen doesn't even exist!" Moon said with a laugh.

"And that we made it up ourselves!" finished Tempest.

"And that the noises they hear are just us, pounding the earth with guanaco skins until we're tired!" replied Sea.

Mountain smiled. "Yes. Thanks to Xalpen they work for us without complaint. Fear is good, my friends!"

The goddesses laughed themselves silly, thinking about their gullible husbands. Sun picked up the guanaco he had hunted and hid it outside the camp. Then he returned to the forest and revealed to the gods what he had seen and heard. Furious, they agreed to surprise their wives just as the hain ceremony began.

The four goddesses were lighting the sacred fire when their husbands arrived. A terrible struggle was unleashed between the gods who had lost their fear and the goddesses who had been discovered. Sun threw Moon into the hearth, where the fire burned her face. All the Howenh suffered great damage that day. To escape one another, they truly became wind and rain, snow and mountains, tempest and sea. Moon fled to the sky with her face burned, which is why the moon is darkened by spots. Sun went in pursuit of her. Ever since, he races across the sky, trying to catch her.

Thus ended the first era of creation on Isla Grande de Tierra del Fuego, the largest Island of the Land of Fire, there at the southernmost tip of the world.

Guabancex

Taino tradition

She lives on high,
where the heavens extend.
She rushes toward earth,
queen of the wind.

Taino goddess,
cemi of storms,
spiraling come
her mighty arms.

Palm trees sway and on the horizon the sea unfurls the most beautiful blues on the face of the earth. Enchanted isles, fragrant with the soft perfume of the palms. Islands that shine like jewels and that some say are the summits of submerged mountains. Warm nights when the moon shines and seems to sing a song that caresses the sand. What could happen to disturb the peace of this paradise?

Suddenly, the sea feels strange. Its blues and greens change hues. The waves seem to weigh more than usual and move slowly, their crests uncrowned by white foam. It looks instead as if a dark and infinite snake is uncurling beneath the surface, almost visible through the darkening waters.

But it is not a snake. It is a goddess, a mighty cemi.

Her name is Guabancex. She becomes enraged if the Taino

people have not treated her well, if they have not made suitable offerings. Then she calls upon her heralds, Guatauba and Coatrisque, and leaves the cave where she dwells—in the country of Aumatex, ruler of the winds—moving swiftly on her one foot.

Oh, Guabancex! Her arms stretch to infinity, spinning in endless spirals until winds rise that can rip up even the most robust of trees and hurl entire houses through the air. The fastest, most agitated of these winds is Hurakan.

Her assistant Guatauba emits terrible groans that rumble through the sky. Roaring thunder that drives the animals crazy and stuns the island folk. And where Guabancex passes, Coatrisque causes the water to rise and spill, to overrun the riverbeds, to flood the land, bringing desolation, disease and misfortune.

Then, her hunger for destruction sated, Guabancex lifts up her arms and returns, exhausted, to the land of the winds.

Guahayona

Taino tradition

On an island
in the turquoise sea
a mermaid lives
within a dream.

For Guahayona
she patiently waits,
to carry him home
upon the waves.

Guahayona lived in a cave, on an island, along with his father and his half brother, sharing the space with other families. They thanked Turey, who is the sky, for giving them life, but a succession of diseases, a breakout of strange sores and the ever-growing number of children with damaged limbs made that life difficult.

Guahayona was a tall and strong young man, his dark skin glittering with golden tones. Though he had not escaped the scars left by the sores, he stood apart from the other inhabitants of the cave and the island for both his beauty and his health.

One night he had a dream: a beautiful woman stood on a rock in the middle of the sea, gesturing at him, singing a sweet song.

The next day he knew what he had to do. He left the safety of the cave, taking one last look at his sick and miserable people before boarding a small boat and launching into the sea.

Ah, the infinite freedom of the waves, the horizon, the vast calm blue. But danger and storms also awaited.

He disembarked on the island of Guanin and saw no one on the beach. He had just sat down to rest in the shade of a palm tree when he saw the woman of his dreams coming toward him, emerging from the sea all dressed in foamy waves. She spoke to him with a sweet and musical voice:

"Guahayona, you've finally arrived. I'd grown tired of calling you, of screaming your name in the wind."

"How did you know that I even existed, and what is your name?" replied the astonished young man.

"I am a cemi, daughter of the sea, possessed of her infinite wisdom. My name, so you always remember, is Guabonito; I am also a healer, tasked with tending to your wounds and giving you the remedy to cure the diseases of your people."

Guahayona spent long months at Guabonito's side, learning all the healing properties of plants. He discovered that the children on his island had damaged limbs because his people did not strengthen their blood with marriages outside the clan. Marriage between cousins was weakening their lineage. Soon his people would disappear.

"And you, wise Guabonito, would you marry me?" the young man asked his beautiful teacher one afternoon as the setting sun bathed the island of Guanin in gold.

"My mission, Guahayona, is simply to reveal to you your destiny as a healer of your people. That I have done. All that is left is for me give you cibas and guanin. Cibas are the stone beads with which the Taino people must adorn themselves and which bride and groom must exchange upon being married. Guanin, which gives our island its name, is a blend of gold, silver and copper.

That alloy has the power to lengthen life. Your people must wear ornaments fashioned from the metal on their chests and calves."

When it was time to leave, Guabonito gave Guahayona leaves of the guayacan tree to prepare healing infusions.

"You take with you my teachings and the memory of my name," she said. "I know you will never forget the days you spent with Guabonito on this enchanted isle."

With a broken heart, because he loved her, Guahayona left the coast of Guanin on his own mission: to heal his people and strengthen their blood through marriage taboos. He bore the guayacan leaves and the cibas and the secret of the guanin alloy. The young man, who had left in pursuit of a voice that called to him in dreams, would soon become the glorious cacique Albeborael Guahayona, who freed his people from sickness and strengthened the blood of the Taino nation.

Hun and Vucub

K'iche' (Maya) tradition

The road that goes down
will also come rising.
Hun and Vucub—
their defeat was surprising.

But those two brothers
knew just what to do.
Their story survives
in the *Popol Vuh*.

In time of darkness, when minor gods walked the earth, there lived two brothers: Hun Hunahpu and Vucub Hunahpu. They were partners in everything, except in marriage. Vucub never married and had no children, while Hun found a wife and had two sons, Hun Batz and Hun Chowen, to whom he attempted to give the best education possible. He made sure they learned to sing, to engrave stone, to paint beautiful glyphs on rolls of bak.

Hun and Vucub loved to play the ball game pokolpok, using any excuse to start a game. One day while playing, they came too close to the land of the dead, a fearful place known as Xibalba.

The lords of the underworld heard them play. Some said to the others, "Why do Hun and Vucub always play on the surface of the earth?"

"We have to invite them to play ball with us down here," still other lords replied.

They all agreed. "It will be a pleasure to beat them so we never

again have to hear all their ruckus or irritating voices above us on earth."

Far away or very close, none other than Hurakan—Heart of Sky—had sent those thoughts to the lords of the underworld. He had also inspired Hun and Vucub to play ball that day so far from home.

Hurakan went to make sure that the lords of the underworld sent four owls as messengers to the surface world to invite the brothers to play ball.

"It is our lords' will . . ." began Arrow Owl.

"That you bring your leather protectors for your hips," One-Legged Owl continued.

"And good gloves," Macaw Owl added.

"But don't forget your rubber ball!" shouted Skull Owl, certain the brothers would not let him speak.

Hun and Vucub looked at each other with worry. They understood what it meant to be invited to play in the underworld. But they also understood they could not disobey and that in the ball game there is always a chance to win.

"All right, owls," Hun said. "But we must go to our house to say goodbye to the family."

"Be quick," demanded Arrow Owl, who always spoke first.

They said their goodbyes. Their mother, Ixmucane, wept for her sons, whose destiny was dark. The brothers consoled her and told her to keep their collection of rubber balls in a special place.

"We promise, Mother, that we will play with them again," said Vucub, kissing his mother on the forehead.

"And you, my sons," Hun said to his children, "behave well and continue to study. Above all, cheer your grandmother's heart."

Ixmucane began to cry even harder. Vucub told her, "Be at peace, Mother. We have not died yet."

Then they were off, leaving behind Ixmucane and the two boys, their house and the world above. Very soon, accompanied by the four owls, Hun and Vucub found themselves on the road to Xibalba. They knew that they would have to pass various tests and escape many traps: such was the reputation of the lords of the underworld.

They found an opening in the ground, surrounded by boulders. Down it they went, coming to a river between steep canyon walls that they crossed with great effort. They arrived at another river with broad pools and many scorpions. It was difficult, but they were astute and managed to cross it. They passed through a river of blood and a river of pus. They were almost celebrating their victory when they reached a crossroads.

Four roads spread out before the brothers: red, black, white and yellow.

The Black Road spoke.

"I am the one that leads to Xibalba. The lords await you both with precious gifts. March down me and you will arrive soon."

The brothers were too tired to think. They allowed themselves to be guided along the road. They almost rejoiced when they reached beautiful, comfortable rooms where the majestic lords of the underworld were sitting on their mats of power. Their expressions seemed to receive the brothers warmly, so Hun and Vucub hurried to offer polite greetings in return.

"Lords of the underworld," Hun said, "may you have the very best of days."

"Hail, Majesties," said Vucub, bowing deeply. "We are grateful and happy that you have honored us with this invitation to your realm."

There followed a heavy silence, thrumming like a bee's wings. Then the silence was broken by wild guffaws. It was the lords of the underworld, doubled over with laughter, emerging from their hiding place. They had tricked the brothers with lifelike wooden figures disguised as themselves.

Hun and Vucub decided not to take offense at the joke. They laughed as well, celebrating the Xibalbans' clever prank.

"Now," said one of the lords, "sit down on these polished benches that we have prepared for you. We will immediately bring you each a cup of refreshing chocolate."

With smiles, thinking about the chocolate, Hun and Vucub sat on the benches.

They jumped up immediately, screaming. The benches were extremely hot and they had burned the unsuspecting brothers.

The Xibalban rulers roared with laughter. This time neither Hun nor Vucub smiled. They understood that they had fallen into a trap, that the Black Road had deceived them, and that the lords of the underworld delighted in causing them harm.

"Oh, but enough of pranks!" said one of the lords. "Enter that house. We will give you lit torches and lit cigars. If you wish to remain alive, then tomorrow you must return the torches and cigars intact, just as we are giving them to you."

And they pushed the brothers into the House of Darkness, the first place of punishment in that wretched underworld. The darkness was so complete that Hun and Vucub could see only the glowing of the torches and the cigars. As they knew that what the lords required of them was impossible, they decided to smoke their cigars and enjoy themselves as best they could, there within the House of Darkness.

"Listen, Hun," said Vucub, "there's no way out. This realm and its lords are too powerful. We're trapped."

"Yes, Brother, I'd noticed," Hun said. "And I've been thinking. We can't do anything, basically. They're going to sacrifice us. No compassion. No ball game. It will be a bit annoying, but we're gods. Minor ones, sure, but we won't actually die. And our children will rescue us. Someday."

The next morning came, just as black as the night. Hun and Vucub left the House of Darkness and appeared before the lords of the underworld.

"Where are the torches?" cried one.

"And the cigars?" asked another.

Hun and Vucub shrugged. There was no point in arguing against such injustice, against creatures so determined to destroy them. When the executioners raised the flint knives to cut off their heads, the two brothers knew for certain that the people of the underworld were heartless and cruel.

Hurakan

K'iche' (Maya) tradition

It's Hurakan,
the biggest is he,
a powerful god,
lord of the sea.
Sweeping the earth
from end to end,
he prepares it all
to start again.
Heart of Sky
spiraling wide,
with only one leg
does Hurakan stride.

Hurakan—whose name in the K'iche' Maya language means "one-legged," also known as Heart of Sky—was summoned by the creator gods to shape new human beings. All the deities surrounded him with the greatest respect because he had always existed, spinning between the immense waters and the endless void. With his only leg, he could travel immense distances in an instant. He also liked to walk upside down, using his hands.

The first human beings, those made of clay, had been a failure. Those clumps of mud could not even stand up without their ears falling off or their mouths twisting sideways. The gods never bothered to ask them to speak. Such a feat would have been impossible. All it took was a little water thrown in their faces and they dissolved completely.

That's why the gods thought of calling Hurakan for a second attempt. Heart of Sky agreed to the task right away, excited to try his hand at creation. After deliberation, the gods decided he should make the new human beings out of wood. It was an excellent idea, because the wooden men and women would not melt away and could stand firm on their two legs.

The beings Hurakan created seemed a success. Even when ordered to speak, the wooden men and women did so quite clearly, and—compared to the mumblings of the mud folk—their speech was impeccable.

They populated the land, having wooden sons and daughters. But through some unseen defect, they never really possessed either minds or hearts. They forgot very soon to thank the creators and never looked upward to revere Heart of Sky. They walked around empty, without meaning or deep purpose. They had many possessions, animals and objects alike, but for all they did and all they owned, their minds were dark.

So Hurakan, Heart of Sky, in agreement with the other gods, decided to destroy his own wooden creation. He descended upon the great waters, spinning upon his only leg. He walked on his hands, surrounded by a whirlwind that lashed the land. He ripped up the buildings of the wooden men and women, destroying their empty pride. Before he laid them to waste as well, he attempted one last time to teach them the error of their ways. But they learned nothing. Their ignorance had no remedy.

He sent dogs and turkeys to seek revenge for all the animals these hollow humans had slaughtered and eaten. He made the pots, the mortars and even the stone griddles come to life and voice their outrage at their owners.

Just as the wooden people had filled pots with ash, ground the mortars and heated the griddles red-hot, so they were made to suffer. The hearthstones in every home leapt up at the same time to hit the wooden men and women, who ran in every direction to save themselves to no avail. They tried to climb the trees, but the trunks bent over to prevent them from escaping. They tried to hide in the caves, but rocks sealed their entrances. Hurakan gave them no quarter. He beat at them with whirlwinds and torrents of rain that fell ceaselessly from the sky.

The days were as dark as night. One by one, the race of wooden people was destroyed.

Ixquic the Maiden

K'iche' (Maya) tradition

Ixquic is here.
Ixquic is there.
She walks forever
everywhere.
From her home on earth
to the world below,

the beautiful Ixquic
can come and go.
Deep in her blood
eternity shines:
immortal Ixquic
is wholly divine.

When the lords of the underworld decreed the execution of the brothers Hun and Vucub, they ordered that they be buried in the ball game court. Then it occurred to them that Hun's head should be hung as a warning among the branches of a tree on the side of the Black Road.

Though all they did was set it there, the next morning, the tree—which had never before borne fruit—was full of higuera gourds, hard and white as skulls. The lords of the underworld were astonished, because they had never seen such things. Among the explosion of flowering fruit, Hun's head could no longer be recognized, since it had become like a calabash too.

As days and weeks passed, all the inhabitants of Xibalba paraded before the higuera gourd tree, astonished at the miracle. The lords of the underworld forbade anyone from cutting the fruit or standing beneath the tree. They understood that the power of the tree to draw visitors came from the presence of Hun's head somewhere in its branches. Without strict control, the place would become a center of veneration.

But a Xibalban maiden—Ixquic, Lady Blood, daughter of one of the lords of Xibalba—could not sleep. She lay awake all night, thinking about the famous tree. She had not been able visit it before the ban, but her friends had told her all about it. So one night, without her father's knowledge, she snuck off to see the higuera gourd tree and to taste its fruit, which rumors claimed was delicious and sweet.

When she reached the foot of the tree, Ixquic muttered out loud, "Will I die if I taste one of the higuera gourds of this beautiful tree?"

To her surprise, a voice answered, "The fruits of this tree are just a bunch of skulls. Do you still want to eat them?"

The young woman was startled. But curiosity got the best of her.

"Yes. That's my wish. That's why I came in secret."

"Extend your hand toward one of the fruits," the voice said.

Ixquic did so, and one of the higuera gourds—Hun's skull, in fact—spat into her hand.

She looked, surprised, at her open palm. The saliva, which she had clearly felt wet her skin, had evaporated. Hun continued speaking, from within his skull.

"My lady, I have given you my essence, my divine immortality. Now go up to earth, look for my mother, and tell her you carry her grandsons in your womb. Be confident, for you will not die: you are protected by a promise. To whoever asks you, say that everything has happened by the will of Hurakan, Heart of Sky. He has inspired us all, both those from the surface world and those in Xibalba, your homeland, dear maiden."

The skull of Hun revealed to Ixquic many more secrets: he told of his brother Vucub and of his sons, who had been left in the care of Ixmucane, his mother, in the land above, and how before leaving for Xibalba they had instructed their mother to watch over their rubber balls, because they would return to use them once more.

But Ixquic returned home instead. After six months her father, a powerful lord of Xibalba, noticed that she was pregnant. Enraged and ashamed of his daughter, he demanded to know who was the father of the unborn child.

"There can be no son because there is no father," Ixquic replied.

"Liar!" cried the powerful lord, who had already asked the other lords of the underworld for advice on what to do with his daughter. "For that lie, you must be sacrificed. Come, messenger owls! Take my daughter and sacrifice her with a flint knife. Bring back only this bowl, her silent heart inside."

The four messenger owls flew off, carrying the maiden through the sky. As they traveled, she explained to them what had happened, that Hun's skull had spat in her hand, that she now carried his essence and divine immortality, that she had to escape to the surface world, leaving Xibalba behind.

"And all this is by the will of Hurakan, Heart of Sky," Ixquic concluded. "So, wise owls, in the name of Hurakan, do not sacrifice me, as my father and the lords of the underworld command."

"You certainly should not be sacrificed," said Arrow Owl, who always spoke first.

"We would never disobey Hurakan," One-Legged Owl said.

"But we must take a heart to our lords," said Macaw Owl.

"We must find a replacement," suggested Skull Owl, who was very thoughtful.

The maiden pointed to a red tree she had seen while flying. They descended, and with the sacrificial flint knife, they cut through the bark. A red sap began to flow, and Ixquic caught it in the bowl. The sap squirmed as if by magic, kneading itself, and soon hardened in the shape of a heart.

The messenger owls took the bowl, flying back to the lords of the underworld. The lords examined it in detail. Some, suspicious, suggested throwing it upon the fire. When they did so, what they thought was Ixquic's heart released an exquisite aroma. All of them inhaled the pleasant fragrance and fell deeply asleep.

While the lords of the underworld slumbered, the owls led the maiden to the surface world.

They left her in front of Ixmucane's house, from where Hun and Vucub had departed to never return and where Hun Batz and Hun Chowen, sons of Hun, had remained to study with the very best teachers.

Ixquic knocked three times on the door. Soon an old woman opened it. The maiden threw herself at her feet and said, "Mother, open your arms to me, for I carry in my womb the essence, the divine immortality, of your son Hun!"

"My sons, Hun and Vucub, are dead. The earth swallowed them whole. How dare you speak to me about immortality?"

"Your sons have not died. They asked you to keep their rubber balls because they would come back. And they will do it through me, your daughter-in-law."

Ixmucane burst into tears. She opened her heart and arms to the brave maiden who had traveled upward along the treacherous roads of Xibalba to bring her hope and promise.

"Your grandchildren, Mother," Ixquic said sweetly, "will return to you the affection of those sons you lost. And if someone asks you how it was possible, just tell them that everything was inspired by Hurakan, Heart of Sky."

Soon afterward, during the long hours of a starry night, Ixquic, the maiden from Xibalba, gave birth to two beautiful twins, whom she and her mother-in-law named Ixbalanque and Hunahpu.

K'awil and the Prince

Mopan (Maya) tradition

Mortal love
is short but sweet;
even the gods,

heaven's elite,
long for the passion
of humans they meet.

In the far-off years at the beginning of this age, the people of the Maya Mountains made treks to sacred caves to perform their rituals and appease their gods.

There was a prince in those lands who ached for love. His father, the king of Uxbenka, told him to visit Naj Tunich, holiest of sites among those heavenly peaks.

"Make your offering at the altar, beside the sacred pool," the king instructed. "Then will the gods fulfill the yearning of your heart."

The prince traveled the miles alone. It was an arduous trek, climbing higher and higher. Finally, at the end of a ravine, a steep cliff wall rose above him. In its center, a hundred feet from the ground, the entrance to Naj Tunich loomed, a dark circle full of promise.

Pilgrims had lifted two great mounds of rock and dirt to near the cave. Steps had been carved into the cliff face to ease the final few yards.

The prince made his way silently into Naj Tunich. The first chamber was long but narrow. Glancing up at a balcony that overlooked the cavern, the prince walked toward the pool of still, clear water that glittered faintly in the sunlight slanting in through the entrance.

Beside the pool stood an altar with a basin. Beyond, in the gloom, the holy Well of Souls gaped like an eager mouth.

The prince drew a maguey spine from his bag and pierced his skin, letting a few drops of blood spatter into the basin. Then he intoned his prayer.

"Lord K'awil, God of Lightning and Magic, hear me! I long to love and be loved. Grant me the affection of the perfect young man, with dark flashing eyes and long supple limbs. I spill my blood in recompense, O Mighty One!"

From the Well of Souls came a low moan. The prince was terrified. But the moan became a chuckle, soft and gentle.

From the well a being emerged, dazzling in beauty save for one strange thing: his left leg was a serpent.

The prince understood. This was K'awil. He fell to his knees.

K'awil had heard the young man's prayer, had looked upon him from the realm of the gods and saw that he was beautiful. It had been eons since the Lord of Lightning had allowed himself to love. This mortal called out to him, body and soul.

"Will a god suffice, young prince?" he asked, sweeping the young man into an embrace.

A kiss was all the answer he needed.

For many years, K'awil and his prince lived in those mountains, their days filled with beauty and love and lore.

But gods never age, though humans do.

The king of Uxbenka fell ill. Messengers came to call the prince home.

Though the mortal man was loath to leave, K'awil kissed him one last time.

"Thank you for giving your heart to me," the god whispered. "But now we both must go. Another love awaits you, one I selected long ago. Ascend your throne. Take a mortal husband."

The prince wept bitterly. "This time we shared . . . it will be forgotten forever."

"No," K'awil said. "Follow me."

He led the prince to the cave of Naj Tunich, through the first chamber, into the deeper, darker levels of that holy site.

There, upon the wall, etched with lightning from K'awil's magic staff, gleamed an unforgettable image.

The prince and his divine lover, locked in sweet embrace.

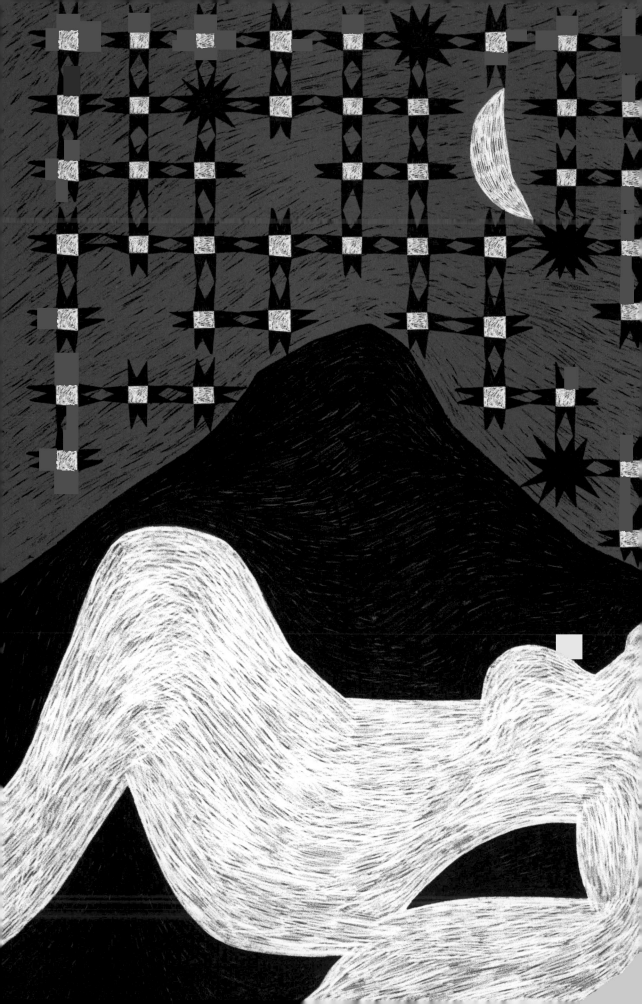

Iztaccihuatl and Popocatepetl

Nahua tradition

She is a princess.   She is mountain.

A warrior, he.   A volcano, he.

The snow is a mantle   A heron will fly,

upon their sweet dream.   a quetzal will sing.

Many years ago, during a time measured by the brightness of the moon and the singing of birds, there was a young woman named Iztaccihuatl: White Maiden. Her father was the king of an important city at the heart of Anahuac, that land of mountain ranges, enchanted lakes and blue skies crossed by the flight of snowy herons.

Iztaccihuatl lived in a beautiful palace of polished stones that builders had erected for the glory of her father and their city. The king was a proud warrior lord who had subdued many neighboring kingdoms. Iztaccihuatl was his favorite daughter, so he delayed finding a husband for her, not wanting her to leave his side.

Iztaccihuatl always wore white and loved to relax in her father's gardens. Listening to the varied voices of the mockingbirds gave her great joy. The iridescent feathers of the quetzals fascinated her.

One afternoon in the gardens, the princess discovered a nest of hummingbirds. It was strange, because these birds normally hide their nests very well. But there it was, in a bush, almost at eye level. The princess stood on tiptoe to see inside. She even dared to bend the branch that held the nest a little. She noticed a pair of white eggs and was already stealthily pulling away when a hummingbird came flittering in front of her with a threatening air. It was so small, yet it spread its wings like a warrior of the sun. The princess was afraid. She knew that she should not have looked into the nest, or bent the branches of the bush that held it. As she walked away, ashamed, her heart grew heavy with a vague premonition.

Days later, a group of young noblemen came to Iztaccihuatl's father's house. They were from an allied city, and had come requesting permission to join his army. The king imposed hard tests of valor on the warriors. Though all of them passed with grace, one stood out from his peers, a young man with intense black eyes and long hair held down by a band around his forehead. Popocatepetl was his name: Smoking Mountain.

In the course of the welcome banquet the king arranged in honor of the youths, the eyes of Iztaccihuatl and Popocatepetl met. The princess felt her heart might burst from her chest, and powerful emotions came over the warrior as well. Throughout the rest of dinner, Iztaccihuatl kept her eyes downcast. Popocatepetl remained silent.

That night neither of them could sleep. When they closed their eyes, each saw the other's face. Love had ignited in the souls of Iztaccihuatl and Popocatepetl. Their days were filled with restlessness and mystery.

The princess could not stop thinking about the haughty warrior. Love stirred in her breast, impatient and bittersweet. She looked for some meaning in the poetry of her people that could comfort her. The words of Nezahualcoyotl, the wise poet king of Texcoco, echoed in her mind like the clear voice of a god:

> With flowers you write, Giver of Life,
> with songs you bring color,
> with songs you sketch the outlines
> of those who must live on earth.
> Then you destroy eagles and jaguars,
> only in your book of paintings do we live,
> here on earth.

Iztaccihuatl understood that her love for Popocatepetl was written by the Giver of Life, that it was part of her destiny, that it would have to bloom. She peered into his own soul, saw herself reflected in it as on the surface of a lake, and felt reborn and happy. Words bloomed from within her, and together with the verses of Nezahualcoyotl, they made her feel like a poet as well:

> The singing does not stop.
> From my spirit come rising
> the features of your face.
> Our story
> is a book.
> A book of paintings
> written with flowers
> by the Giver of Life.

A short time later, the king, who had noticed what was happening between the two young people, sent for Popocatepetl. Iztaccihuatl had been summoned as well. She sat in a low chair next to her father, who wore the majestic regalia of the monarchs of those lands.

"Popocatepetl, you are the bravest of my warriors, the most outstanding. I wish you to remain forever among us. To that end, I offer you the hand of my daughter Iztaccihuatl."

The girl went pale. She had had no idea of her father's plan. Popocatepetl felt immensely happy, for he longed for the sweet princess with all his heart. He was about to reply when the king, with a gesture, instructed him to keep quiet.

"But in order for this arrangement to be fulfilled," the king continued, "and for you to show yourself worthy of my daughter, you must carry out a feat of war. A hundred days of travel from here, there is a fierce city that refuses to submit to my rule. Its king has challenged my authority, ignored my power, and dishonored my messengers, executing them and sending me their severed heads as a sign of his contempt."

At that moment, a servant of the king entered with a tray upon which lay the gruesome spectacle of three severed heads. Iztaccihuatl covered her face with her hands.

"You must lead a war party against that city and return with the head of the enemy king on the tip of your spear. Then you will become my heir and my daughter's husband."

Popocatepetl departed the next day with his army. He carried with him a flower that Iztaccihuatl had given him during their brief encounter that morning, during which they had confessed their mutual love.

"Promise me that you will return," the young woman had said, "that you will keep yourself alive in this war my father is making you wage."

"I will," replied the warrior. "And you, Iztaccihuatl, promise to wait for me."

The road to the enemy kingdom was long. Long as well was the siege of the city. The war that followed was unavoidably cruel. After grueling battles and the loss of many good men, Popocatepetl finally defeated the monarch and faced the gruesome duty of cutting off his head and mounting it on a spear, as Iztaccihuatl's father had ordered.

While this war was being waged, however, the king changed his mind. He decided that it would be better to marry Iztaccihuatl to the lord of a neighboring kingdom whose wealth would increase the royal treasure. Having received no news of Popocatepetl and losing interest in getting revenge against a distant kingdom, the king told his daughter that the young warrior had died. As she stared in shock, her father explained that a different marriage would be arranged as soon as possible.

Waves of loss overwhelmed the princess, effacing all joy and hope. She fell ill and lay in bed for nine days and nights. On that ninth evening, a hummingbird came flitting through the window and hovered over her head before flying away.

The next morning, the king's servants found Iztaccihuatl dead.

Deep pain shook the entire palace.

As fate would have it, Popocatepetl returned victorious that afternoon, the head of the enemy king mounted on his spear.

When the warrior learned of the death of his beloved, he thought he would go mad with pain. Before anyone could stop him, Popocatepetl took the princess in his arms and climbed a high mountain with her. When he reached the top, he laid her gently on the ground, arranging her hair and the folds of her dress. Iztaccihuatl seemed to be asleep; death had only heightened the beauty of her face.

Popocatepetl knelt beside her, determined to guard her body forever.

That night, the gods of Anahuac sent a fine and constant snowfall that covered the bodies of the two youths, turning them into volcanoes.

Ever since, Iztaccihuatl lies with her hair extended, covered with snow, silent.

Beside her, Popocatepetl reminds us with quakes and eruptions that he is still waiting for his princess to awaken.

Heart of the Mountain

Nahua tradition

Sun of earth	Tezcatlipoca,
and sun of wind:	smoking mirror,
a rivalry	and Quetzalcoatl,
that brings the end.	lord of the air.

There was a time when the earth was populated by a race of mighty giants. It was the first age of the world, lit by a sun of luminous darkness that was also the supreme god, no less mighty than the giants: Tezcatlipoca. His color was black. Black his feathers, black his regalia. His emblem was a smoking mirror, a polished disc of obsidian from which curled smoke, mist, haze.

The giants amused themselves by tearing up trees with their hands, as if blades of grass. They also emptied the rivers, sucking up the waters with their mouths. They bit the mountains, leaving caves behind. When they performed their war dance, stamping the ground with their massive feet, the earth shook and the seas trembled.

Tezcatlipoca burned and shone through the long night of his reign over his civilization of giants. But the cosmos needs balance,

so this age had to end, its dark sun of chaos had to go out, the world had to die in order to be remade. So from the East came Quetzalcoatl. His color was white. White his feathers, white his regalia. In his hand, he carried a curved staff, which he could use to whip up thundering tornadoes, dizzying waterspouts.

Quetzalcoatl rushed through the cosmic night and with the power of his staff defeated Tezcatlipoca, knocking him from the sky and dragging him to the depths of the sea. A few minutes, or centuries, or millennia later—time in that age was not measured as it is now—an infinite roar thundered through the universe and from the ocean a huge jaguar emerged.

Oh, Tezcatlipoca! His skin constellated with stars, his leap shocked heaven itself. From mountains and caves, from the underworld, from the very night sky, countless jaguars sprang into being. They crossed the world and devoured the race of giants, because that people's time had come to an end, as the age of the sun of earth was fulfilled.

The god of the smoking mirror, in the form of a jaguar, took shelter in the most remote of the caves. He became Heart of the Mountain, Tepeyollotl, of spotted fur and rumbling voice. So he lived during all the years and centuries and millennia of the reign of his enemy, Quetzalcoatl, the sun of wind.

When the dual god decreed the end of the sun of wind, the Tezcatlipoca in jaguar form was entrusted to destroy it. With a leap that stunned the very stars, the Heart of the Mountain knocked Quetzalcoatl from the sky. A strong wind arose that hurled the god of the curved staff and his people far away, to a place without name or stars, without earth or ocean.

Ball Game

K'iche' (Maya) tradition

The court, the rings,
their pads and ball—
to play this game
they risk it all.

The Hero Twins
use all their wiles
in Xibalba
to pass the trials.

One afternoon, the brothers Hunahpu and Ixbalanque found the rubber balls left behind, as a promise, by their father, Hun, and uncle, Vucub, in the house of their grandmother, Ixmucane.

When the twins saw those dusty spheres, their hearts roiled with joy and grief and rage—but above all, with a consuming yearning to play pokolpok. They left the house and found their family's ball court, almost devoured by the jungle. The twins cleared the field, carefully sweeping the floor and preparing to play.

They had been passing the ball up and down the court for a few minutes when, in the underworld, the lords of Xibalba heard the stomping and thudding sounds over their heads. Almost immediately they knew what was happening in the surface world. They were indignant.

"How dare these twins play ball where once their father and uncle disturbed our rest?" some demanded.

"We must summon them to play in Xibalba!" others insisted.

The lords of the underworld laughed, thinking of all the traps they would set for the twins, luring them to death as they had done with Hun and Vucub.

They sent the four messenger owls to summon the brothers. The winged heralds found Ixmucane alone, sweeping the house.

"The lords of Xibalba send us," said Arrow Owl.

"We're looking for your grandsons, Hunahpu and Ixbalanque," One-Legged Owl explained.

"They have been summoned to play ball in Xibalba within seven days," clarified Macaw Owl.

"In addition to a ball, they must bring their own gloves and leather hip pads," Skull Owl concluded.

Old Ixmucane was devastated when she heard the news. As she had so many years ago, once again she had received a message of death.

When Hunahpu and Ixbalanque heard the news, they showed the same strength as their father and uncle, consoling their grandmother as best they could.

Hunahpu said, "Grandmother, we'll leave two stalks of corn planted in the center of the house. Through them you'll know if we're still alive."

"If they dry up, Grandmother," explained Ixbalanque, "it means we've died in Xibalba."

"Even if they do, they might bloom again," Hunahpu hurried

to add. "That would mean we finally beat them at ball."

The brothers began their journey to the underworld and crossed the rivers of water, blood and pus that their father and uncle had once crossed. When the Black Road rose up, inviting them to travel along it, the twins smiled. They had devised a plan.

They soon spotted the lords of Xibalba, assembled together, waiting for the brothers in majestic poses. The brothers sent a mosquito ahead to test whether these were the true lords or wooden decoys.

The statues, because that is what they were, did not flinch at the bite of the mosquito. The lords of Xibalba, annoyed because their ruse had not worked, came out of hiding. The mosquito bit them one by one, causing them to screech with pain.

Hunahpu and Ixbalanque laughed and laughed.

Nursing their mosquito bites, the lords then invited the twins to sit on the stone benches they had arranged for them.

"Those are not benches," said Hunahpu.

"No. They've been heated by fire," Ixbalanque agreed. "If our legs get burned, we couldn't play ball as you've commanded, Majesties."

The brothers laughed again as they stared into the perplexed faces of their hosts. Without any urging, they walked over to the House of Darkness, ready to spend the night before the game. The lords gave them a lit torch and lit cigars, commanding that they deliver them intact the next morning.

Once inside the brothers immediately put out the flames. Instead, they attached the red tail of a macaw to their torch. At the ends of their cigars they placed tiny fireflies that shone like stars.

At dawn, the surprised lords of Xibalba received the torch and cigars intact. They had no choice but to recognize that the twins had passed all their trials.

This time there would be a game.

The masters of the underworld would find it very hard to win.

Kukulkan

Yucatec and K'iche' (Maya) tradition

Feathered Serpent,   of the stars,

Heart of Sky,   of the rivers,

both creators   of the cornfields

of the heavens,   and the roads.

Before anything in existence—creatures or objects—in an infinite night that contained within itself the seeds of all the days and suns of the world, the two creators met. One was Hurakan, Heart of Sky, the other Kukulkan, Feathered Serpent.

They parlayed for eons, exchanging divine words until they reached an agreement to create the world.

In that cosmic darkness, the creators began. First they would say a word, then things emerged into existence. They said "kab," and the earth was made, appearing from the center of a cloud, a roiling thick mist, a formless fog. They said "witz," and from the waters the ranges rose, surging upward while gathering their skirts, rivers running forever down their slopes, water seeking a way back to the sea. The creators said "k'ih tyee'," and from the earth burst forth trees, their green leaves providing precious shade on white-hot days.

Kukulkan was content. He said to Heart of Sky, "We have done well, Hurakan. The word has become the world. And the world that we have created is beautiful. But we have to fill these broad, open spaces with beings that move and glide, that feed and sleep. We must give the mountains their faithful guardians."

The two creators then fashioned the animals: deer and snakes, jaguars and pumas, owls and quetzals.

They assigned each species a place to live and rest. The deer along the rivers, the birds in the boughs of the trees.

The creators sat on mats of cloud to contemplate the world, delighting in its beauty. Speaking almost as one, Hurakan and Kukulkan commanded the animals:

"Speak!"

Neither the jaguars nor the quetzals, neither the owls nor the deer could pronounce a single word. They roared, hissed, squawked and howled, but neither Hurakan nor Kukulkan could distinguish even the faintest echo of an intelligible word in the language of the gods.

The creators then took dirt in their hands and molded human beings. Two legs, two arms, an elongated face and haughty forehead. But something was wrong. Their work was defective. The men and women of the dirt melted at the slightest rain and could not utter a single word with their sad mouths.

They went on to carve beings of wood. These could move and talk, but they soon revealed their hollow nature. As men and women with empty minds and ungrateful hearts, they never gave thanks for having been created.

Beings so poor in spirit, so lacking in desires and ideals, did not deserve to exist, decided Hurakan, decreeing their extinction. Strong winds and storms swept the wooden beings away. The only ones that managed to survive were those Kukulkan transformed into monkeys. With time they forgot they had ever been human.

The creators withdrew into the cosmic night to think about how to fashion intelligent beings that deserved the generous gift of life, that could wield words in powerful ways. Heart of Sky hid himself in the midst of the darkness, while Feathered Serpent uncoiled his long body to rest upon a mountain range.

In time, the coyote and the fox, the parrot and the raven brought before Kukulkan yellow grains in the shape of delicate ears. The four animals showed the Feathered Serpent the magical hill where these grains were hidden.

Kukulkan shuddered with understanding, his feathers shining, his scales gleaming. At that moment, regarding the hill and the bounty it contained, he knew that human beings must be made of maize. Only then would language take root in their minds, blossoming into poetry.

Kuyen

Mapuche tradition

Antu is the sun,
Kuyen, the moon.
They both arose
from the misty gloom.

And since then,
they shine on high
like two jewels
hung in the sky.

Once there was eternal night, without time or stars, darkness vast.

In it slept Pu-Am, the spirit. His infinite eyelids closed, the whisper of his breathing was the only sound, like the rustling of the sea when it is calm. Nothing happened, nothing occurred, nothing moved. There was no hate, but neither was there love.

Then, Pu-Am woke up. He opened his eyes and spoke the first word of creation. At his command, other spirits arose: the Pillan, male gods of nature, and the Wangulen, the beautiful stars above.

The most powerful of all the Pillan was Antu, the bright sun. The most beautiful of the Wangulen was Kuyen, the splendid moon.

Antu announced to the assembly of Pillan and Wangulen that

the next day he would select one lovely light among all the stars to be his wife.

Every Wangulen wished to be the chosen one of Antu. They embellished their glow with adornments and glitter.

Night came to a close as dawn filled the horizon. Rising bright and majestic in the sky, Antu chose Kuyen as his wife.

The moon now traveled through the night dressed in white, ermine feathers entwined in her black hair. Her beautiful face shone, for she was Antu's consort. Love came into being, also a dream of the great spirit, Pu-Am. Forever would the sun follow the moon in her circuit through the sky. Forever would Antu love Kuyen.

But Antu's choice gave rise to sadness and envy and disappointment too. These emotions gripped the other Wangulen, who hurled aside their ornaments and flowers, the white feathers of their hair. Feeling rejected, the stars began to weep. Streams of water flowed from their eyes, forming the rivers and lakes that, upon the mountaintops, became snow.

The wedding of Antu and Kuyen took place, and the stars wept even more, until their tears formed the trackless seas.

The Pillan of the sun, angered by all the bitterness that the Wangulen had poured out on his wedding day, punished them by dimming their brightness. As their light flickered and nearly went out, the stars begged forgiveness of the sun.

Antu took pity on the Wangulen and restored part of their brilliance. Ever since, starlight trembles, tenuous, in the heavens, a reminder of not just the sun's punishment, but also his mercy.

Brighter than them all, of course, shines the chosen one of Antu's heart: his wife, the beautiful Kuyen.

Llorona

Nahua and colonial tradition

When they call you Llorona,
they know the reason why—
your grief is so great,
it's no wonder that you cry.

Llorona, if you'd let me,
to give you joy and peace,
I would take you in a boat
and sail across the sea.

She emerged from the lake where the city of Tenochtitlan sprawled. The appearances occurred at night, during the reign of the great lord Moctezuma.

A woman dressed in white, her face veiled by the mist. The Mexica saw her and heard her cry with a pain so deep that it shriveled one's soul.

Many denied her existence, claiming that her voice was but the howling wind, her dress the light of the moon as it filtered through the trees.

The wisest among the Mexica said that she was Cihuacoatl. The time had come, they said, for the goddess to give Quetzal-coatl the bones of the dead to form humankind once more.

But she kept on weeping and crying out as it was said the cihuateteo did, those women who had died in childbirth and who sometimes appeared at the crossroads, harbingers of death.

"Oh, my children!" people claimed that she screamed. "Woe to my children! Children, my children, where shall I take you!"

Hearing that lament, other learned elders believed that this was not Cihuacoatl, or one of the cihuateteo, but Tonantzin, the divine mother who cried for her children, for those who had been born and died too young, and for those who had died in the womb.

Time passed and the sun of the Mexica faded. Emperor Moctezuma died and the conquerors transformed the city of Tenochtitlan into the capital of New Spain. They drained the lake, and for a few years, the lament was not heard again. The woman in white did not reappear. Cihuacoatl and the cihuateteo fell silent. Tonantzin wept no more. Another era had begun.

Canals became cobbled streets, echoing with horseshoes. The churches rang mass, and the tolling of the bells sent their melancholy upon the air.

A young Mexica girl had married a Spanish soldier. She changed her gods and her language for those of her husband, giving him three children whose faces displayed the union of two races. Within a few years, however, the soldier—like many other Spaniards in his situation—abandoned his indigenous wife to arrange a marriage with a woman from his homeland.

Deep sadness seized the young woman. A fountainhead of tears opened in her chest, and she was tortured by her thoughts. She loved her husband, yet he had abandoned her and her little children, who would now grow up without a father.

She no longer felt the will to live. Her soul had been crushed. One night she woke her children and led them through dark alleys to the ancient whirlpool at Pantitlan, where not so many years before the Mexica had sacrificed children chosen by the goddess of the waters. With no tears left to cry, the young woman pushed her children into those depths, then crouched on the shore, watching the whirlpool.

There the sentries found her the next morning, stiff with cold, her eyes glassy. They took her to a court that sentenced her to death. But she didn't care. The pain she felt, her longing for her children, was greater than any fear.

A few days after the execution of the young indigenous woman—whose plight had moved many hearts in New Spain—the first reports arose of people claiming to hear again, at crossroads and late at night, the almost forgotten lament:

"Oh, my children! Children, my children, where will I take you!"

Aakulujjuusi and Uumarnituq

Inuit tradition

In the cold lands
of the northern expanse
a woman dug deep
in the ice with her hands.
She made a great hole
and out leapt the animals,
source of food and clothing
for her people's survival.

Behind the caribou,
she saw a bright flash—
a mighty white wolf,
which after them dashed.
There are some deaths
that make a herd strong.
You'll discover it's true
as you read along.

When everything began in that beautiful land of ice, what we now call Alaska and Canada, the first two humans emerged from mounds of earth on Igloolik Island, both of them men. Their names were Aakulujjuusi and Uumarnituq. In time, they fell in love.

One day, Uumarnituq's belly began to grow, and the gods revealed that he was pregnant with Aakulujjuusi's child.

"How will he give birth?" Aakulujjuusi cried, his heart heavy with worry.

"I will teach you a spell," a voice whispered from all around. It was Silla, oversoul and breath of life, the universe itself.

Once he had learned the sacred words, Aakulujjuusi knelt beside his sleeping beloved and chanted the spell.

"Inuk una, usuk una, paatuluni nirutuluni, paa, paa, paa!"

Divine magic wrapped itself around Uumarnituq, a glowing cocoon. When the light faded at last, he had become a woman.

So was the first child born, through boundless love and transformation.

In that distant age, there was neither sun nor moon, nor ice upon the sea. It was a world of perpetual summer, but continual night as well.

Aakulujjuusi longed to hunt, to bring back meat to his wife and son.

But Uumarnituq understood the price to be paid. "Let it remain dark forever, dark and warm. Should dawn ever break, the cold will come."

Her husband could not stop dreaming of the hunt, however, so Uumarnituq at last relented.

"Very well. Let it dawn."

The sun rose, illuminating the world. Then clouds covered its face, bringing gloom and snow and ice that clogged the waters.

Strangely content, Aakulujjuusi started off on a journey, searching for other living beings. He left his wife alone.

Uumarnituq sat down to think things through. What would her husband hunt in such a barren and icy world? She decided that it would be best to ask Kaila, the god of heaven, to populate the earth.

"What did you say?" the god's voice rumbled through the vast blue above her.

"We are very alone, my husband, my child and I. You should make creatures, other than humans."

"Do you mean animals?" asked Kaila.

"If you say so," answered Uumarnituq, who of course did not know what the animals were as she had never seen one.

"Since you're the one asking, you have to collaborate," Kaila said from above.

"Of course. What do I have to do?" asked Uumarnituq.

"Open a hole in the ice beneath your feet. Make it a big one. You're going to be very surprised."

Uumarnituq did as Kaila asked. When the hole was finished, she saw water and, in the water, bubbles. Within moments she had reached down and pulled out a fish. Afterward a seal emerged from the hole. Then a partridge and an elk and an eagle and a bear . . .

"And now," Kaila said, "my special gift. It will feed your children and your children's children. With their skins you will make the warmest, lightest clothes and build cozy summer homes."

From the hole Uumarnituq had made leapt a caribou, shaking its haughty antlers.

Kaila fell silent off in his blue sky. The woman sat quietly too, deep in thought.

Sometime later, Aakulujjuusi returned with a caribou over his shoulder. He told his wife what he had seen: a land full of animals that ran, flew and swam! Uumarnituq smiled and said nothing.

Over the years, Uumarnituq and Aakulujjuusi had more children, and those children had children. As Kaila had promised, they hunted caribou and wore those skins to fight the bitter cold.

As time went by, however, humans abused the hunting ritual, killing the most beautiful and robust prey. In consequence, only skinny and sick caribou remained alive. Their meat was not enough to feed the people, not to mention their skins, which were useless.

Uumarnituq, now old and wiser than ever, decided it was time to speak once more with Kaila and remedy the situation.

"It's very simple," Kaila said from the sky. "Go back to the hole you dug, all those years ago. In your excitement, you didn't pull out all the animals. One remains."

The first woman returned to the place where she had dug the hole. Ice had formed but it broke with ease beneath her hands. Soon, the bubbles rose again.

From the hole emerged a beautiful white wolf.

"He has sent me Amarok, spirit of the wolf," whispered Uumarnituq in awe.

And to this day, wolves devour weak and sick animals, keeping healthy and strong every herd of caribou, that gift of the sky god to the Inuit people.

Mayahuel

Nahua tradition

That beautiful plant
beneath the mesquite?
The spiny maguey—
with a tale honey-sweet

about Lord Quetzalcoatl
and lovely Mayahuel.
Their love was condemned
by the stars as they fell.

In ages past, when gods walked the earth, a young woman named Mayahuel lived with her grandmother. Mayahuel possessed a rare beauty; her hair was black as night, her eyes green as still lakes or precious emeralds.

Mayahuel's grandmother was one of the ferocious Tzitzimimeh, a fallen star who had become a sorceress on earth. She raised her granddaughter with a very firm hand. From morning to night, she made Mayahuel do housework, never giving her time to rest. Every time the young woman expressed a desire to leave the house to walk among the trees, her grandmother prevented her. The old sorceress watched her fiercely—if she had been able to get into the young woman's head, she would have also controlled what and how she thought.

On one occasion, the great lord Quetzalcoatl went flying

above the sea-ringed world, carried aloft on wings of wind. He happened to alight near the house where Mayahuel and her grandmother lived. There he saw the young woman looking out a window, sighing with the yearning she felt to go outside.

The girl's beauty moved Queztalcoatl. He drew closer, hovering outside her window.

"Do you want to come with me?" he asked simply.

Mayahuel, herself enthralled at the sight of Quetzalcoatl, replied, "Yes, but my grandmother won't allow me to leave the house."

"It doesn't matter what your grandmother says. What counts is what *you* want," said Quetzalcoatl, taking her by the hand.

A few minutes later, they had walked deep into the heart of the forest. Quetzalcoatl took Mayahuel in his arms, and at his touch, they both transformed into a beautiful tree with forked branches and roots that sank deep into the ground. A gentle wind stirred its leaves, and the rocking boughs seemed to caress each other. Birds came to perch on the enormous tree formed by the union of Mayahuel and Quetzalcoatl.

At night, the old sorceress discovered that Mayahuel was not asleep on the rough mat that was her bed. She went outside and looked up at the sky. With a terrifying scream, she called to her sisters, the Tzitzimimeh:

"Sisters, to me! What I feared most has happened. My granddaughter has run away!"

The Tzitzimimeh dropped from the sky like a dazzling meteor shower. When they touched down upon the earth, they took the form of old hunchbacked witches, with hooked noses and gnarled hands.

All went in search of Mayahuel, arriving together at the clearing in the forest where the young woman and Quetzalcoatl had merged their souls into a single tree.

But when Mayahuel saw her grandmother arrive—followed by her gruesome aunts, the frightening Tzitzimimeh—she pulled her head away from Quetzalcoatl's embrace to scream in terror. The tree split in two, and the grandmother recognized the silhouette of her granddaughter in one of its boughs. Rushing toward her, the fallen star seized the thick branch with her claw-tipped fingers and ripped it away from the divided trunk, shredding it as she screamed at the other old women:

"Sisters, to me! Come and devour my traitorous granddaughter! I've found her, hidden in a tree. Let justice be done!"

The Tzitzimimeh scurried to her side and began to devour the wooden remains of Mayahuel. Soon their bellies were full. When they left, bits of shattered branches and leaves were scattered all over the clearing.

Meanwhile, the half of the tree that was Quetzalcoatl had remained intact, its branches upright and proud, its roots still gripping the soil. He regained his lordly form and contemplated with infinite sadness the remains of Mayahuel. He took them lovingly in his hands and buried them, in the same place where he had embraced her, in the same place where the fearsome Tzitzimimeh had carried out their vengeance.

Not long afterward, from the bits of Mayahuel's body buried by Quetzalcoatl, the most beautiful of plants sprouted: the green maguey that stretches its arms toward the sky and from whose heart women and men extract aguamiel, the sacred drink.

In each of the magueys that grows beneath the stars across this sea-ringed world, Mayahuel forever lives and remembers forever the love of Quetzalcoatl.

Monetá

Muisca tradition

Siramena's dance
spins and weaves.
Flutes trill a song
of joy and peace.

Moneta's voice
intones the song.
The sky rains hope
upon the throng.

The Muisca people living in towns near the immense dusty
wasteland of Boyacá had always lived among anxieties.

The continuous drought made them thirsty while diseases
afflicted them.

As if such calamities were not enough, every night a fireball
crossed the sky, crashing into a massive pit that had formed in
the dry, cracked ground. Then terrifying noises echoed through
the darkness and the earth shook.

"It's Busiraco," said the Muisca people. "The monster, the
snake, the evil dragon that feeds on fire, breaking up the clouds
and driving away the rains."

Some had seen Busiraco and had gone mad from the sight.
Prophecies claimed the beast would destroy humanity and that
he had chosen to start in that dry and dusty place because it
suited his fiery nature so well.

In those days, a holy man named Moneta walked among the
living. He had been trained by the wise Bochica in the principles

of civilization and had become a leader among the people. He wore an emerald around his neck that Bochica had given him to transfer to Monetá his status as holy man.

Monetá knew that the town was thirsty and lived in constant fear of Busiraco. He wanted to remedy their situation, so he began fasting and meditating, searching for the best way to end the drought and fear.

At last, he understood what he would have to do. He summoned the people to gather. To his side he called Siramena, a priestess renowned for her deep spirituality, who followed the teachings of Bochica. Together they raised their arms to the gathered people to ask for silence.

When all were still, Monetá said, "The god Chiminigagua wants to save you from thirst and misfortune. Through me, he communicates his will: we have to make a great pilgrimage through the dusty lands to the Temple of the Sun in Suamox. There we will render tribute to the goddess of water, Bachué, the blue-eyed."

The trek was long and difficult. When the Muisca people reached the Temple of the Sun, Priestess Siramena performed a dance that seemed to sketch worship in the air while the drums and flutes sounded. Siramena wore white, her hair loose. As she spun, her hair whipped through the air like a storm, promising rain. Around her neck swung a gold disc from a chain, sparkling magically in the sun.

Monetá asked everyone to bow their heads and close their eyes. At that moment, Siramena lifted the gold disc as an offering to Bachué and hurled it into the gaping pit not far from the temple. Right then, Busiraco was squirming, deepening the drought, awakening fear in every Muisca heart, flinging disease into the air.

The disc slammed into the beast's head, splitting it in two. Busiraco twisted violently, his enormous tail beating the earth. But in seconds his massive body lay stilled, slain by Siramena's perfect aim. At that moment upon the heads of the people whose eyes were closed, drops of beneficent water began to fall.

Bachué had accepted their offering! The people smiled in joy. Many lifted their little children into the air to receive the blessing of the water.

Only then did Monetá removed the emerald he wore around his neck. Hefting it as an offering to the Sun, to Bochica and to Bachué, he hurled it with all his might into the heart of the dusty wasteland. As it struck the ground, the emerald was transformed into a fountainhead from which precious liquid began to bubble and spread, iridescent green, glinting in the sunlight. It did not stop until a huge lagoon had formed, occupying the entire wasteland, sealing that cracked earth under tons of water.

This, the Muisca people know, is the origin of Lake Tota, the largest in Colombia, from blue-green waters that burst forth from the emerald of Monetá.

Nahual

Nahua tradition

Behold your nahual,   Some secret force
your best friend—   or animal
by your side   that can travel far:
until the end.   faithful nahual.

After the creation of the sun and the moon, there in Teotihuacan, Quetzalcoatl knew that only he would be able to go down to Mictlan, the land of the dead, to collect the bones of the ancestors with which he would fashion new human beings.

But he recognized that even he, powerful as he was with the force of the wind that stirred the beautiful quetzal feathers of his headdress, could not do it alone.

So he summoned his nahual, his double, to accompany him on the dangerous journey. Once they had passed the terrible tests to reach the heart of Mictlan—mountains that slam together to crush travelers too slow to pass between them, a hill bristling with blades, a wind full of flint knives, whirlwinds that strip away flesh and a heart-eating beast—Quetzalcoatl and his double at last arrived at the center of that frightful realm.

While his nahual awaited him in the shadows, Quetzalcoatl appeared before Mictlanteuctli and Mictecacihuatl, the sovereigns of Mictlan.

These chief gods of the underworld have no skin. In the depths of their eye sockets stars dully glow. They adorn their skeletal forms with precious jewels, marigolds and pleated paper cones. Headdresses of black plumes crown their skulls. They sit majestically in obsidian thrones, surrounded by their favorite animals: the bat, the owl and the spider.

Without wasting a second, Quetzalcoatl spoke to the lords of the underworld:

"I come seeking the precious bones that you guard. With your permission, I will go gather them up."

Mictlanteuctli, eye sockets lit by a chilling blue fire, demanded, "And what will you do with them, O Quetzalcoatl?"

"Create. I will fashion new men and women. We gods of heaven want to ensure that someone lives on earth."

Mictlanteuctli fell silent. A devious plan occurred to him, a way to deceive Quetzalcoatl.

"Very well, Feathered Serpent," he said at last. "Blow my conch trumpet while walking four times around our realm."

The lord of death extended his conch to Quetzalcoatl. Immediately, the wind god realized the trumpet was not hollow. It could make no sound. Concentrating his divine energy, Quetzalcoatl summoned worms to bore two holes in the great shell. When they were finished, bees arrived, entering the conch to blend their buzz with the god's breath. The resulting sound echoed throughout Mictlan.

Mictlanteuctli was enraged that Quetzalcoatl had defeated him, but hid his feelings and said in a very dry voice, "Take the bones, Feathered Serpent. You have earned them."

Once the god of the wind had left to find them, the king of

death immediately gave a command to the inhabitants of Mictlan, that nation of shadows that eternally inhabits the underworld:

"My subjects, all of you at once! Tell Quetzalcoatl he must leave the precious bones where they are."

And all the spirits, gods and monsters in Mictlan shouted with one voice:

"Quetzalcoatl, leave the precious bones where they are!"

"I will," exclaimed the Feathered Serpent; but in a low voice, he called his nahual out of its shadowy hiding place.

"Beloved nahual, of course I will take those precious bones with me. But pretend to be me, my double. Go to show the shadow folk who inhabit this place that you will leave the bones where they are."

So the nahual did. Everyone was convinced the precious bones would not leave the underworld.

While his double was deceiving Mictlan, Quetzalcoatl had already collected the bones of man and woman, separating them carefully, bundling them up.

The eye sockets of Mictlanteuctli glowed suddenly bright with infernal fire. His courtiers trembled. They had never seen him so angry.

"People of Mictlan, we cannot allow Quetzalcoatl to mock us in this way. All together, now! Dig a great pit into which Quetzalcoatl will fall and break his legs!"

His subjects obeyed. When Quetzalcoatl approached with his bundles of bones, they released some quails to walk between his legs and make him fall. Quetzalcoatl dropped to the bottom of the deep hole, breaking his legs and back, dying a divine death there in the land of the dead. The bones of the ancestors were shattered as well. The quails pecked and gnawed them further, till the ancient remains were nothing but fragments.

Because of his great spirit, because of his quetzal soul, the Feathered Serpent came back to life, rising and walking with great stiffness, like someone traveling from far away. He stared in horror at the destruction done to the bones. He grieved, shedding tears and calling his nahual.

"What should I do now, my nahual? The bones are shattered, pecked to pieces. How can I make humans now?"

The nahual, as afflicted as Quetzalcoatl, said, "Though everything has gone wrong, we must press on."

Quetzalcoatl and his nahual collected the fragments, separating again the bones of the first man from the bones of the first woman. Bundling them up, the two headed for Tamoanchan, the place of origin, paradise on high.

The gods and goddesses were gathered, hopeful for a new human race. They lamented to see the bones broken, but nothing could be done about it.

Suddenly inspired, the goddess Quilaztli emptied the precious load onto her metate and ground the bones into flour.

"We must do penance," she declared, "so that what was broken can be made whole."

Quetzalcoatl approached, piercing his skin with a maguey spine and shedding his blood onto the bone flour. Somber, the other gods and goddesses did the same.

Quilaztli shaped the dough into human beings. Thus were born the men and women of the sea-ringed world. Their descendants called themselves macehualtin: "those earned through penance." For indeed Quetzalcoatl and his nahual had suffered for them, and all the gods of Tamoanchan had done penance to see them live.

Nanahuatzin

Nahua tradition

In the holy city
of Teotihuacan,
the gods all gathered
to create a new sun.
Tecuciztecatl
started to squirm,

the cowardly god
was afraid to burn.
So Nanahuatzin
stepped into the fire,
became the Fifth Sun
that shines in our sky.

Deep in the very distant past, there was a god called Nanahuatzin—the blistered one—because his face was covered with pustules. He was poor, humble and kind, always offering sacrifices to the Giver of Life. He set aside the shiniest maguey spines to pierce his thighs, spilling a bit of his blood to show his devotion.

Nanahuatzin and the other gods survived the cataclysm that ended the Fourth Age. It had rained so much that the sky itself had collapsed in pieces onto the earth. When the waters receded, they found themselves in a depopulated and dark world. They agreed to gather in the great city of Teotihuacan to create a new sun.

When midnight arrived, they lit a bonfire in one of the squares of the beautiful city. And there, the gods said, "Who will sacrifice themselves for the sun to rise?"

A gallant and rich god, Tecuciztecatl, proclaimed in a powerful voice:

"I volunteer, O Gods!"

And with determined steps he headed for the bonfire. But when he felt the flames crackling near his flesh, he succumbed to fear and backed away. He tried twice more with identical results.

The gods frowned. Tecuciztecatl had failed. Soon the fire would go out and no sun would emerge at all.

The gods said again, shouting in anguish and anger:

"Who will sacrifice themselves for the sun to rise?"

"I am unworthy, but I volunteer, O Gods."

And from the farthest end of the Avenue of the Dead, Nanahuatzin came running, his broken sandals tied to his feet with rough rope. His awkward running became a blur, and he flew into the bonfire. There the brave god began to burn; he heard his flesh sizzle and pop, yet he was consumed without a groan.

Ashamed at his cowardice, Tecuciztecatl leapt into the flames of the bonfire, which consumed him as well.

The gods set out to wait for the new heavenly lights. They did not know whether they might emerge in the North, South or West. But it was in the East that they saw the birth of the sun that was Nanahuatzin, followed by another sun that was Tecuciztecatl. The gods threw a rabbit at the coward so that he shone less brightly. He became the moon.

However, the sun and moon sat wobbling on the horizon, unable to rise any farther. The gods understood that all of them, without exception, would have to sacrifice themselves.

Wordlessly, the gods stepped into the dying flames of the bonfire, lit by their own hands there in Teotihuacan. Their divine energy flowed into heaven, pushing both sun and moon into motion.

The Age of the Fifth Sun had begun.

Ñamandú

Guarani tradition

Where's that beautiful
land without harm?
Please, Ñamandú.
Tell me, Tupa.
Where the breezes
all smell of the sea,
where there is no war,
just lasting peace.
It's the destiny
of the Guarani
to feel fulfilled,
to be happy.

In the remotest of times, before anything was, a dense fog filled the cosmos. Without heat or cold, without shape or color, stirred by the breath of constant winds. In one moment of that primal chaos, the stirring fog shuddered more than usual: Ñamandú had just created himself.

From the beginning, in Ñamandú was the word.

From the beginning, in Ñamandú was the soul.

Because soul and word are one and the same.

That is why, almost immediately, Ñamandú spoke to himself:

"What do you most want, Ñamandú?"

"To be a father of gods."

"And then?"

"To create the earth."

"For what purpose, Ñamandú?"

"So that my most beloved children can live there."

"Who will be your most beloved children, Ñamandú?"

"Human beings. The Guarani."

Thus reassured by his soul-word, Ñamandú went on to create his first children, the gods. Before anyone else, he gave rise to his son, Py'aguasu, or Great Heart, god of words and good conduct and divine love. Later, he created Karai, master of fire and bright sunlight. His third son was Jakaira, mist and smoke, constant companion of the flame. His fourth son was Tupa, the pleasant freshness of seas, lakes and streams, whose clarity makes the earth livable. This last son was so good that throughout the millennia he naturally became the successor of Ñamandú. The Guarani people directed their prayers and songs to him.

Once the first earth had been created—resplendent with blue palm trees, the favorites of Ñamandú—it was populated by human beings who faithfully followed the dictates of Great Heart. Although they had to endure extreme temperatures and the fiery rays of the sun, due to Karai's nature, they also enjoyed the soft mist that descended from the mountains as Jakaira commanded. When they felt overwhelmed with fatigue, they were renewed by the fresh and beneficial breath of Tupa, which put joy and vitality in their hearts.

"As long as they continue like this," said Ñamandú to his soul-word, called Ayvú in the Guarani language, "respecting the rules dictated by Great Heart, they will enjoy a golden age. And it could last . . . forever."

"The freshness of Tupa will always help you," replied Ayvú, "but don't forget that human beings, your beloved Guarani, chosen and brought by you to the world, have desire in their hearts, though it be small. If that desire ever goes against what Great Heart dictates, it could offend our divine nature."

Ñamandú did not answer, perhaps because he already knew what would happen. One day the Guarani did indeed offend the gods by following some of their errant wishes. The golden age could no longer be. Ñamandú sent a flood, dividing the earth into two parts: the Land without Harm, place of unattainable eternal life, and the New Land. The second still retained its blue palm trees, mountains and rivers. But something had been lost. It was too earthly for those Guarani who remembered the golden age.

"Soul-word," said Ñamandú, "dear Ayvú, let's play with these little human beings, to whom we once gave a land without harm and who now must live in this new yet harmful land, which we ourselves have created."

Ayvú was going to answer from Ñamandú's heart, but to the ears of both came the voices of the Guarani people, pronouncing such beautiful words, in such a fluid and musical language, that the creator found himself smiling for joy.

"We want to go back!" the Guarani sang. "Gods, give us back our true nature as beings destined for fulfillment and happiness, truth and beauty! We will not rest until we return to our beloved Land without Harm, where we once lived and can never forget."

Since then, the Guarani people in Brazil, Paraguay, Argentina and Bolivia have not stopped looking for ways to recover that home for which they yearn: Yvy Mara'ey, the Land without Harm, where they will become, someday, the divine beings they were at the beginning of the world.

Ñandesy

Guarani tradition

With bits of moonlight
and the wind's gentle lay,
Ñandesy was born
from the gods' pot of clay.

She suffered great sorrows
and brutally died.
Then she, Our Mother,
was brought back to life.

Ñamandú had created first himself, then other gods and finally the first earth, but he realized that he did not have a wife.

He went for a walk around the world. Smiling, he found he loved the dense forests, the immense rivers through which beautiful snakes endlessly flowed, the multihued orchids with delicate perfume and the spotted pelt of the fearsome jaguar.

Contemplating the earth, solaced by its beauty, he came upon the god Ñanderu Mba'ekuá, Our Wise Father. Between the two they discussed the need to create a woman. It was Ñanderu Mba'ekuá who proposed to mold a clay pot, and both gods went to work. From their hands emerged a container they carefully sealed with a lid.

They were not sure what would happen; they simply followed their impulses as creators. The clay they had used to mold the pot had trapped fragments of moonlight and the murmurs of song the wind intoned among the trees. The gods covered the pot and waited for an entire night.

The next day, Ñamandú lifted the lid. Before his gaze and that of Ñanderu Mba'ekuá emerged a woman so beautiful that both gods forgot to breathe. Without speaking, because they had not yet given her speech, she stared with newly opened eyes at the two gods. Each felt the caress of that gaze.

"You will be called Ñandesy—Our Mother," said Ñamandú, taking her to a mountain crowned with blue clouds, where he made her his wife and gave her the gift of speech.

But Ñanderu Mba'ekuá had also fallen in love with Ñandesy. One day, when Ñamandú was off on a long journey through the Guarani lands, the other god traveled to the mountain of blue clouds and asked the woman to become his wife.

Ñandesy accepted. She saw no harm in the love of Ñanderu Mba'ekuá, who had also created her. But when Ñamandú returned to the mountain and learned what had happened, sadness overwhelmed him. His disappointment was so great that he left Ñandesy and the blue clouds forever.

In time, nostalgia for Ñamandú seized Ñandesy. She could no longer bear to live in the mountains. Every alcove reminded her of how happy she had been with her first husband. Also, she realized that she was pregnant and thought that the news would cheer Ñamandú. So she did not hesitate: she abandoned the security of her abode and set off barefoot to search the world for her husband.

Poor Ñandesy! She did not get far. A pair of hungry jaguars sensed her shy step. Leaping from the trees, they knocked her down and feasted on her sweet flesh.

So it was that, ahead of time, Ñandesy's twins were born. Because she had been loved by her two creators, the dying woman brought into the world two children: the son of Ñamandú and the son of Ñanderu Mba'ekuá.

The brothers survived thanks to the wise grandmother of the jaguars, who set aside her beastly impulses to raise those boys she sensed were divine.

A long time later, when Ñamandú decided to recover his beloved Ñandesy, using the power of his word, he resurrected her and led her back to live in the blue mountains crowned with sky. When the twins grew and set out in search of their mother, Ñamandú turned his son into Our Father Sun, and the son of his rival into Our Father Moon.

White-faced Bear

Alutiiq (Sugpiac) tradition

Mighty hunter!
Think, if you will,
when some bear
you wish to kill.
If it's a mother
there with her cubs,
just let them live;
don't spill their blood.

Hunting for pleasure?
It's a mistake,
for there is a bear
who'll make you pay.
Take no more
than what you need:
anything else
is just evil greed.

Qat'sqaq was the most prominent bear hunter in his village. At first, his friends admired him, but over time, seeing that they could not match him, they began to feel an unhealthy envy toward him. They plotted to ask a powerful shaman to turn him into a beast.

The shaman liked the request. It would be a challenge for his magical arts.

"You must kill a bear," he told them, "then remove its skin and place it, without his noticing, under Qat'sqaq's bed."

The hunters felled a good-size beast and skinned it. Then, led by the shaman, they entered Qat'sqaq's hut when he was gone, and hid the skin under his bed.

The next day, when Qat'sqaq awoke, he found he had transformed into a huge bear with a white face and paws.

"The white marks will let you know which bear is Qat'sqaq," the shaman had told the other hunters.

Qat'sqaq went to the tundra to live like a wild beast. He became the most ruthless destroyer of men, giving them no time to shoot their arrows or throw their axes. Once he had ripped them apart, he would examine the remains as if searching for someone.

Many years later, in another village, a young man began to stand out in bear hunting. His name was Panaq and he was constantly risking his life. His friends, worried, begged him to spend less time on the hunt because he would soon run into the dreaded white-faced bear, which would destroy him without mercy.

"They say he is a man who was transformed into a beast by the shaman of the neighboring village. So he has sworn revenge on the human race that wronged him with magic," they explained.

"I'm not afraid," Panaq replied, "and if your advice inspires anything in me, it's the desire to kill every bear that crosses my path."

A few days after this conversation, Panaq left his village and entered the tundra, intent on finding the white-faced bear to show as a trophy to his friends.

Instead, he found a large mother bear with her two cubs.

Maybe I shouldn't kill this bear, he mused at the sight. *She's not the beast I'm looking for. Besides, her cubs would be unprotected. Even I have my limits.*

Just then, the bear reared up in a threatening stance, wanting to protect her cubs. Panaq instinctively nocked his bow, loosing an arrow with deadly aim and striking the mother bear right in the heart. The cubs fled in terror, and the hunter dragged the carcass to his village.

His friends shook their heads in disapproval.

"You're offending the race of bears," they said. "Soon they'll seek revenge, and the white-faced bear will come for you. Straight to your house it will go."

This did nothing but stoke the fires in Panaq's heart. The next day he left in search of the fearsome bear. After a week of travel, having consumed all his provisions, he arrived at a stream rich in red fish. Thinking that bears would arrive soon to catch their food, he waited all day and all night. He never sighted one of the animals, so he decided to move, still confident in his instincts. Around noon, he reached a cliff from which he spotted a large group of bears gathered in the tundra.

His heart pounded when he saw a huge creature with a white face and paws.

Hours passed. Panaq did not abandon his lookout. He was studying the movements of the magnificent bear, who seemed to be the chief of the others. On the one hand, the young hunter marveled at its beauty; on the other, his desire to kill it grew.

When the sun went down, the bears left the place where they had spent the day—all but the bear with a white face and paws, who now assumed a menacing posture, staring at the place from which Panaq was watching.

In some inexplicable way, within a few seconds the bear was standing in front of him.

"Is nothing enough for you, bloodthirsty man?" he growled. "Were you not satisfied killing my wife, leaving my children without a mother? I should kill you right now, break you into pieces, rip off your skin . . . But you're not the man I'm looking for. I will let you live in exchange for a promise: starting today you will never again kill a single bear."

Trembling like a blade of grass in the wind, Panaq fell to his knees, put his face to the ground and cried out:

"I promise!"

When he sat up, Qat'sqaq had disappeared.

Back in his village, the young hunter told everyone what happened with the dreaded white-faced bear. His friends figured he had learned his lesson, but after seven days, the incorrigible Panaq made a proposal to six young men of the village: travel with him to the site within the tundra where he had discovered the gathering of bears.

"We will kill seven," said Panaq. "One for each hunter."

The young men accepted and accompanied Panaq on his foolish trek. Upon arriving at the site, one of the hunters spotted the white-faced bear. Fearful, Panaq abandoned his plan, telling the hunters there was a better spot. He led them to the stream of red fish. Luck was on their side: they discovered a group of seven bears that had come to feed.

A few minutes later, all of the beasts lay sprawled on the ground, dead.

The hunters were preparing to drag the carcasses back to their village when the huge white-faced bear reared up before them, that dreaded beast of the massive white paws. Panaq snatched up his bow, but the bowstring snapped, whipping against his face.

The other hunters tried to shoot the bear, but all their arrows missed.

"Why are you trying to kill me?" Qat'sqaq roared. "What harm have I done to you? Your leader here killed my wife and left my children without a mother. I let him live once, but he has broken his promise. Now I will tear him apart. But I will do nothing to you, for the moment, if you run."

The six hunters rushed away, not giving a moment's thought to the fate of Panaq. The young hunter was to get what he deserved. Desperate to save himself, he begged the bear to grant him only one more night of life to return to the village and say goodbye to his people.

"I will grant you not only one night, but your entire life," said the bear to Panaq's surprise, "if you take me to the man who changed me into a beast."

"Yes, of course," said the hunter without hesitation. Together they made their way to the shaman's hut, where the old man slept peacefully.

The bear ordered Panaq to enter the hut by cutting through the leather door with his knife. They entered and stood before the shaman, who sat up in bed, terrified.

"If you don't give me back my human form," the bear roared, "I will kill you right now."

The shaman struggled all night to turn the bear back into a human. Finally, he managed to peel off his skin. From it emerged Qat'sqaq, his human body somewhat wrinkled.

"I ask you to give me the skin," said the shaman. "It will be of little use to you now."

"Agreed," Qat'sqaq replied, cutting the head and paws of the skin off with an ax. "But I will keep these parts."

Qat'sqaq left, satisfied to be a man again. But first he gave Panaq a warning:

"You may hear rumors that the white-faced bear still roams the tundra. Understand me, boy: do not be tempted. If you ever hunt a bear again, I will kill you without mercy."

At first, the young hunter seemed to have learned his lesson. But not even a month had passed when two of his friends asked his help. A nearby village had sighted a bear. Its face and paws were white. Intrigued, Panaq could not resist. He agreed to their request.

"This time I will have no mercy on you or your friends," the huge bear roared when the hunters nocked their bows.

With inhuman speed, Qat'sqaq, the white-faced bear, killed Panaq and the other hunters, burying their remains with his white paws.

Then he entered the tundra. No one ever bothered him again.

Oxomoco and Cipactonal

Nahua tradition

The very first couple,
the first human beings.
She is our grandma,
and grandpa is he.
They are the origin
of all that we know;

the wisdom that heals us,
the plants that we grow.
She's Oxomoco;
he's Cipactonal,
purest of heart,
ancient and soulful.

Oxomoco was the first woman. Cipactonal, the first man. Quetzalcoatl wanted both to be wise, so he and the other gods shaped them as an elderly couple. The gods gave Oxomoco threads and a loom, and Cipactonal they commanded to work the land.

Never be idle, the first humans were told. The gods also trained them as healers; together they created the art of medicine. They learned the inner workings of time itself, becoming the first astrologers.

Their lifetimes came just after Quetzalcoatl had defeated Mictlanteuctli, taking the bones of the dead to the gods gathered in Tamoanchan. Oxomoco and Cipactonal came into existence that day.

The gods realized they had to find food for their creatures. Quetzalcoatl saw a red ant carrying precious corn kernels and decided to follow her. They arrived at the Tonacatepetl, or the Mountain of Plenty. There, Quetzalcoatl transformed into a black ant, slipped through a crack in the slopes and found himself in a cave full of maize.

Carrying as much as he could, Quetzalcoatl returned to Tamoanchan. With the grain, the gods fed the first humans so they could grow and get stronger. The couple, delighted at the sustenance, asked the gods how they could always have the food of Tonacatepetl.

But the gods had no idea. Quetzalcoatl made an attempt, wrapping a massive rope around the mountain and trying with all his might to drag it into heaven. The mountain would not budge. So the gods sat down to ponder their options.

Then Oxomoco and Cipactonal, putting into practice the skills the gods themselves had taught them, cast lots to see the future. Oxomoco took nine grains of corn and threw them on the ground in front of Cipactonal. The two studied the pattern for a moment and nodded to each other.

"Only Nanahuatzin—that humble god with boils on his face—will be able to crack open the mountain," they declared, "and give corn to humanity."

Nanahuatzin was summoned. With the help of the red, yellow, white and blue tlaloques—gods of thunder and lightning—he burst the Mountain of Plenty open, spilling maize over the entire sea-ringed world.

Since that amazing moment, whenever gods or people needed advice, they asked the wise grandparents, Oxomoco and Cipactonal.

Xochipilli and Xochiquetzal

Nahua tradition

Flower Beauty,
Flower Prince:
two halves of a whole,
a flower from whence

music and art
and love arise—
no matter the gender
they welcome your sighs.

At the beginning of time, the Dual God—Ometeotl, union of female and male in one two-spirit being—unfolded into other deities to begin the difficult work of creation.

Sometimes, those unfolded children were like their parents: dual beings that could assume one aspect or the other, but that mostly existed in two-spirit form.

One of these divinely double beings created flowers and poetry, song and dance, games and art, love and desire, especially that exquisite longing between two people of the same gender.

But the time came when they had to divide, to become distinct. Omecihuatl, the female half of the Dual God, took a strand of her hair and gently split her doubled child in two.

Their male aspect was Xochipilli, the Flower Prince.

Their female aspect was Xochiquetzal, the Flower Beauty.

What was the need that prompted this split?

A child had been born at last upon the earth. Oxomoco and Cipactonal, the first man and woman, had brought a son into existence. They named him Piltzinteuctli, Beloved Young Prince.

The boy grew into a man, but there was no woman on the earth to be his wife.

Xochiquetzal, now fully female, looked on Piltzinteuctli and found him lovely. They married, living happily for a time in those early years of the cosmos, the world wide open and ripe for exploring.

After many years, on a Seven-Serpent day, Xochiquetzal bore a child, a demigod, two-spirited like their mother and grandparents. Chicomecoatl, the parents called their newborn. Seven Serpent, like the day of their birth.

When the baby began to crawl and toddle, corn burst from the earth every place their hands and feet pressed into the soil. The gods rejoiced, for the divine source of maize had arrived, and humanity could finally begin to spread throughout the sea-ringed world, its sustenance assured.

Chicomecoatl later discovered their own complementary halves.

Xilonen was the young goddess of green and tender ears of corn.

Cinteotl was the older god of dried maize still on the cob.

As the dual demigod of corn matured into their sacred mission,

Xochiquetzal felt a yearning to return to the paradise of Tamoan-chan and reunite with Xochipilli.

Her husband, Piltzinteuctli, also felt a yearning. He had begun to run through the wide expanses of the sea-ringed world, content and free beneath the glorious sun.

Understanding that their happiness was taking them along different paths, Xochiquetzal transformed her husband into a deer on a Seven-Flower day. He shook his mighty antlers and pawed at the earth in thanks before leaping into the woods to pursue his own destiny.

Then Xochiquetzal returned to Tamoanchan and embraced Xochipilli at last.

They melted together once more, two spirits joined in one beautiful whole.

Xochipilli and Xochiquetzal became simply xochitl. A single flower.

Some people in this sea-ringed world are special too. That flower blossoms in their hearts.

Xochihuah, we call them.

They who have the flower.

Pacha Kamaq

Andean tradition

Tremors by the river.
An ancient god,
Pacha Kamaq,
groans and shivers.
But time just flows;
the past is past.
A condor flies
while sighing echoes
in the valley
of Pachacamac.

Pacha Kamaq created the first man and woman. He put them in a cruel, arid and dry land, where they could only dig up roots to eat. It was not long before this hard existence ended the man's life. The woman was left alone, grieving and hungry. One day, raising her eyes to the sky and seeing nothing but the Sun, she fell to her knees and addressed a shuddering prayer to the burning orb.

"Lord! You illuminate the world and all things! Surely you see the reason for my sad existence, the source of my loneliness. Could you send me some comfort and hope?"

The Sun took pity on her and spoke with comforting words:

"Better days will come, daughter of the earth. You will smile again, finding beauty in the world. For now, though, you must stay digging up the roots that keep you alive."

The woman did as he asked, and the Sun enveloped her in his rays. From that light, she conceived a child of the sun god, a

little boy who made her smile and opened her eyes to the beauty of life.

But Pacha Kamaq, in his terrible role as the god of life and death, grew jealous of the Sun's child. Without considering the pain it would cause the woman, he killed her son and cut his body into pieces.

"Why would you do such an atrocious thing, Pacha Kamaq?" demanded the woman, grieving once more.

"So that no one on earth will ever go hungry. This way you will never ask the Sun for help again," replied the god coldly.

And he sowed the dead boy's teeth so that corn would emerge. He planted ribs and bones, and yuccas emerged. Fruit trees sprouted from the child's flesh. Pacha Kamaq's words became reality. No one on earth went hungry.

But this bounty gave the woman no comfort. Every bit of food reminded her of the son she had lost. Once more she asked the Sun for help, and once more he had mercy on the woman. With his soft golden voice, he said, "Where is the sprout that emerged from our son's navel, the one that Pacha Kamaq forgot to sow?"

The woman pointed to the dying bit of green. She had been so distressed she hadn't really noticed it before.

The Sun smiled and gave life to the sprout. A beautiful newborn appeared in his arms, and he handed the boy to the woman, saying, "His name will be Vichama."

The woman smiled again. The beauty of the world glowed in her son's luminous face. Vichama grew up healthy and strong, a handsome young man who, like his father the Sun, wanted to travel and know the world. One day he kissed his mother, who had become old, and left, thirsty for adventure.

It was then that Pacha Kamaq learned the woman had raised

another child of the Sun. Anger filled his being. When he could not find Vichama, he took his anger out on the woman, killing her violently, feeding parts of her body to the condors and the vultures. However, he hid her bones and hair by the seashore.

His anger sated, Pacha Kamaq decided to create many new men and women to inhabit the world. He appointed chiefs and caciques to be the leaders of others and to organize the world into kingdoms.

Not long after, Vichama returned. When he did not find his mother, he became enraged and swore to take revenge on whoever had killed her, even Pacha Kamaq himself. He first looked for his mother's bones and found them by the sea. He aligned them carefully and looked for her hair. Arranging it with love around her skull, Vichama—a powerful god who had inherited from his father the Sun the ability to infuse life—resurrected his mother and hugged her against his chest.

Pacha Kamaq understood that his time had come to an end. Vichama was young and strong and would have no mercy on him. To save the little life he had left, the old god let Vichama chase him into the sea. Then, slowly, he eased from those waters, up the Lurin River, and into a nearby valley. When humans finally settled in that place, they named it Pachacamac, after the god who ruled the valley. They erected a temple in his honor.

And every time the earth shudders with an earthquake, they know it is the old creator god, reminding us he still lives, having escaped the revenge of the child of the Sun.

Shepherd and Maiden

Andean tradition

A humble shepherd,
watching his flock,
fell in love with a beauty
out on a walk.

Their love was forbidden
by the stern laws of men,
but magic is stronger
and forever they live.

Once upon a time, there was a shepherd named Acoyanapa, who was in charge of caring for the white llamas destined for the worship of the Sun in the Yucay Valley. He was a graceful young man who liked to play the flute, teasing such sweet sounds from his instrument that the very birds stopped their flight to listen to him and the streams forgot to flow just to catch the beautiful melodies of the shepherd musician.

Near the place where he took care of the llamas was the palace of the ñustas, maidens consecrated to the Sun, the most beautiful young women of the Tahuantinsuyo. They had been separated from their families as young girls, their lives dedicated to that purest of beings, whose heart brimmed with light and jealousy. If any of the ñustas happened to fall in love with a mortal man, she was sentenced immediately to death.

Beyond that danger, the girls enjoyed a bright and luxurious life. Their guards allowed them to take long walks outside the palace, on condition that they return each night.

One day, the most beautiful of the ñustas, Chuquillanto, was strolling with her best friend through the green meadows of the valley when they accidentally came across Acoyanapa, faithfully taking care of the llamas.

When the young man saw them, he fell to his knees, overcome by their beauty. The girls seemed the very embodiment of the crystalline fountains of the Palace of the Sun, famous throughout the region. They could not understand why he was so flustered, so they simply asked after his llamas.

"They are well, thank you," said Acoyanapa. "And you? Are you by any chance the beautiful spirits of the fountains?"

The ñustas laughed, showing teeth so white and perfect that Acoyanapa was convinced they were both divine.

"Nothing like that," Chuquillanto said. "We are daughters of the Sun and, therefore, rulers of the entire world, together with our sisters; but otherwise, we are as human as you, shepherd . . ."

"Acoyanapa," said the young man, standing at last.

The afternoon passed quickly amid the laughter and conversations of the young people. At sunset, the shepherd asked permission to collect his llamas, and the three of them left, the ñustas to their palace and the shepherd to his hut.

The guards checked to make sure the maidens were not carrying anything strange on their clothing, as it was their duty to preserve the purity of the Palace of the Sun.

That night, Chuquillanto had no appetite for dinner. Instead, she retired to her beautiful chambers, closing her eyes to think about the shepherd. For she had fallen in love with the young man, and her heart was a prisoner, sighing in its cage. When she was finally able to sleep, she dreamed of a nightingale that perched on her lap and asked her what she most wanted in the world.

"The love of the shepherd, Acoyanapa," Chuquillanto replied in dreams.

"He loves you too," said the nightingale.

"Really? But our love can never be!" moaned Chuquillanto. "My father the Sun would kill me if I eloped with my shepherd through the Yucay Valley."

"Not all is lost," said the nightingale. "Go stand in the midst of the four crystalline fountains and sing the love song of your heart. If the fountains move in time with your song, then your wish will come true."

Chuquillanto woke up. The dream had been so real she did not hesitate to dress and walk, in the middle of the night, through the hallways of the palace until she reached the place where the four crystalline fountains flowed. Clearing her throat, the ñusta sang in a sweet voice:

> Pitiful me,
> child of the sun.
> Pitiful me,
> if I could but run.
> If I could but look
> as he leans on his crook

one final time
at my shepherd's eyes.

To Chuquillanto's joy, the four fountains swayed to her song, lifting their voices with hers, a harmony as clear as their waters.

The ñusta felt her heart bathed in golden light. Certain she had the protection of the fountains, she returned to her room, where she soon fell into a deep and restful sleep.

For his part, the shepherd tossed and turned in his bed there in that humble shack, unable to sleep a wink. Chuquillanto's figure returned again and again to his memory. The brightness of her eyes, her perfect teeth, her smile. The shepherd kept biting his nails. How had he dared lay his eyes on a daughter of the Sun?

He jumped from his bed, taking up his flute and drawing from it melodies so sad that the rocks of the Yucay Valley began to weep. The melancholy sounds of the shepherd's soul wended their way through the night and reached the ears of his old mother, a fortune-teller who knew at once that she should visit her son before he died of grief.

Before leaving her house located in the Lares Valley, the old woman grabbed a magic staff, as tall as a man, to wield if necessary. She walked all night and reached her son's hut at dawn. Acoyanapa lay on his bed, his face bathed in tears, deathly pale. The old woman woke him, and when he saw his mother, he burst into cries of pain. She consoled him as best she could before going off to search the rocks for nettles, the plant the old ones swear can ease a broken heart.

Nettles in hand, she began to make a stew. At noon, just when she was about to serve her son, the two ñustas appeared at the door of the hut. Chuquillanto and her friend were surprised to see the old woman, who explained she was the shepherd's mother.

A huge smile crossed the lovestruck ñusta's face. Clearing her throat, she spoke kindly:

"Mother, we are daughters of the Sun. As the walk from the palace is long, we are hungry. Could you spare us something to eat?"

"It just so happens that I've prepared a nutritious stew. Come on in, dear girls. This hut is humble, but you will not be denied food."

Without the ñustas noticing, as they fussed delicately at the door, Acoyanapa's mother hid her son inside the magical staff that leaned against the wall.

Chuquillanto and her friend ate heartily, all the while looking for the shepherd as discreetly as possible. The ñusta supposed that he was tending to the llamas of the Sun. When she noticed the staff, it caught her attention.

"Pardon me, but what is that?"

"A very old staff," said Acoyanapa's mother. "And very special, let me tell you. Many years ago, so many that I've lost count, I was a young woman as graceful as you. The great and fearsome Pacha Kamaq fell in love with me, making me one of his wives. When he left forever, driven into the ocean, he left me this staff as an inheritance. But it is already very tall and heavy, difficult for the hands of an old woman to handle. If you accept, I would be honored to give it to you as a reminder of your visit to the shepherd's home."

The ñustas were delighted with the gift. After the meal they set off for the palace, disappointed that the shepherd had never arrived. Chuquillanto carried the staff. Crossing the rolling hill-sides that led back to the Palace of the Sun, she leaned on the staff and sweet feelings washed over her.

At the door, the guards examined them, taking a careful look at the staff on which Chuquillanto leaned. They agreed it was exquisitely carved from the finest wood, so they allowed her bring it inside with her.

The two young women greeted their fellow ñustas, dined sumptuously and finally retired to their chambers to sleep. Chuquillanto took the staff with her and laid it on her bed. When she lay down beside it, she began to cry, remembering the shepherd and thinking that her visit to the hut had been useless. After all, she had not obtained what she most longed for: the chance to see him. A tear dripped onto the staff, which began to shudder. To the girl's surprise, from its ancient wood emerged the beloved form of Acoyanapa, who hugged her sweetly. Then the two kissed deeply amid their tears.

The next day, the shepherd returned to the staff and the ñusta left the palace, this time without her friend, because she had decided to escape with Acoyanapa. Her solitude made one of the guards suspicious. He followed her secretly. Great was his astonishment when he saw, at a bend in the road, a man emerge magically from the staff and hug the ñusta tenderly. The guard cried out in alarm, and the lovers ran as if their feet had sprouted wings. At last they arrived at the edges of the town of Calca. Fatigued by their flight, they fell deeply asleep in the shade of a boulder.

A tumultuous sound awakened them. Coming up the road were the guards of the Palace of the Sun, followed by a shouting mob ready to punish the ñusta's betrayal. Half-asleep, the lovers stood. She took in her hand one of her sandals, her ushuta, the other still on her foot. He looked at her in awe, as one might the most beautiful landscape of Tahuantinsuyo.

And in those poses, by some ancient magic of fountain or staff or nameless gods, the shepherd and the maiden were turned into stone statues so their love could endure forever, untouched by the injustice of men.

Quetzalcoatl

Toltec (Nahua) tradition

He is the snake,
the feathered quetzal;
he flies on the wind,
he smells of copal.

On his chest he bears
the conch, wind jewel.
Lord Quetzalcoatl—
creation he rules.

His father was Mixcoatl, Cloud Serpent; his mother Chimalman, who conceived him after swallowing a bit of jade. Born on the day One Reed in the year of that same name, he was known as Ce Acatl Topiltzin—Our Beloved Prince One Reed.

Lord Quetzalcoatl incarnate.

He had barely reached adulthood when an embassy of lords from Tollan, capital of the Toltec empire, went to Mixcoatl's house to ask about his son.

"The books of destiny say that your son, mighty Cloud Serpent, is to be our king, our lord."

"That he must rule in Tollan, the great city."

"And that under his rule, the Toltec people will reach the highest levels of dignity and artistry, the highest degree of expertise."

"The books also say . . . Ah, Cloud Serpent! You must not learn such things, nor should Ce Acatl Topiltzin. It is not wise to reveal too much of the designs of the Lord of the Near and the Nigh, the Giver of Life, the Inventor of Men."

So the prince abandoned his abode to take possession of his king's mat in the luxurious palace of the city of Tollan, crowned with clouds.

Then came an era of happiness and work. Temples were lifted that would astonish the sea-ringed world. Houses were built with precious stones and iridescent shells, some with walls of exquisite feathers, houses that seemed ready to fly.

Under his reign, corn was plentiful, squash were enormous, the cotton they planted burst from the ground already dyed in every hue. The skies teemed with birds of bright plumage and songs so sweet they caressed the soul. The avenues of cocoa trees were endless, and the great lord of Tollan, Ce Acatl Topiltzin Quetzalcoatl, found so many reasons to thank the creators that he raised a special temple in which to do his own penance. He offered his blood by pricking his thighs with green gemstones.

Inspired by the power of his penance, he outlawed human sacrifice throughout the realm.

Then, from the deepest recesses of the blackest night, from the farthest point of the vault of heaven, a very fine thread came spinning down. It was a spider's thread, and along its length descended Tezcatlipoca, lord of chaos, determined to do everything possible to destroy Ce Acatl Topiltzin, to make him abandon the throne of Tollan, to force him to leave forever.

Tezcatlipoca took the form of an old wizard. He appeared in the middle of the king's private sacrifice, in the peaceful atmosphere of the temple, when Ce Acatl Topiltzin was offering his blood and butterfly wings to the creators. Interrupted in the midst of his pious act, the king felt compassion when he saw the elderly intruder. "The old," he told himself, "are sometimes impertinent, but we owe them respect for all they have lived through."

"Why have you come, dear father, to my palace, to this temple where I offer sacrifice?" he asked, peering down from above, where his luminous thoughts circled in flight.

"My son, the creators have sent me with a task for you," Tezcatlipoca replied in the trembling voice of those who have entered the deep cavern of years.

"What is this task?" asked Ce Acatl. "I am ever disposed to fulfill the will of the creators."

"They asked me, my son, to show you your body."

The king of Tollan shuddered. It had been years since he had looked upon himself, not even his own reflection. Understanding himself to be divine, he now thought of his flesh as irrelevant.

"I must obey, father, for I have promised. But how can I see my body?"

Silently, the old wizard searched among his clothes. He took out a polished obsidian mirror, using necromancy to enlarge the disc until it was as tall as Ce Acatl Topiltzin Quetzalcoatl.

And the king of Tollan looked. First he discovered the wrinkles on his face, eyes bleary with age, dust and sun. He noticed his thinning hair, sunken cheeks, the worn skin of his chest, his flabby belly, his weak muscles. He closed his eyes, realizing his ugliness was an affront to the creators and his own subjects. He was *human*, not divine.

Without a word he turned away from the mirror, left the temple grounds, and confined himself to the darkest room of his beautiful abode.

Tezcatlipoca smiled and rubbed his hands. He had crushed the spirit of the king with his trickster mirror, his devious obsidian that accentuated a person's defects and that, at night, roiled with chaotic smoke.

The king of Tollan refused to leave the shelter of his royal suite. His servants, afflicted, asked the wizard how they could make their lord emerge again, to give orders and direct the worship of the gods.

"Dress him in the divine robes of Quetzalcoatl," Tezcatlipoca said. "Take him that headdress of feathers, the mask of green jade, coat his lips with red pigments, draw yellow lines on his cheeks. Around his neck hang the colorful red feathers of the holy quechol bird."

So the servants did, and the lord of Tollan again felt beautiful and dignified, godlike in his bright colors and feathers, bejeweled and magnificent.

But a sadness had settled in his heart. He confessed his unease to the old wizard. Tezcatlipoca then saw an opportunity to get rid of the king once and for all. With a smile, he explained that all the ailments the king might suffer could be cured with the magical drink he offered. At first the lord of Tollan mistrusted the brew, but he was finally convinced when he took the first sip. His senses relaxed, he loosened his clothes, laughing and dancing with clumsy, ridiculous gestures. He had his servants bring his sister, the beautiful Quetzalpetlatl. The two got drunk and lost their wits, forgetting to do penance, acting like fools.

The next day, when he awakened, Quetzalcoatl's heart was so sad, so repentant, that he broke his feathers and shattered his jades and headed east in search of Tlillan Tlapallan, the mythic Land of Black and Red.

The trek took many years. Along the way he shared his wisdom and gave his name to the places he visited.

Arriving at the celestial shore of the divine water—on the day One Reed in the year of the same name, a full fifty-two years since his birth—Quetzalcoatl wept before getting dressed with the insignia of his rank: his feathers, his mask of green jade, his wind-and-conch jewel. He swore with clenched teeth he would return one day, in another One Reed year, to set the world right again.

Then Ce Acatl Topiltzin set himself on fire, brave lord, god made flesh. Immediately his ashes rose to the clouds, where they were greeted by the tribe of precious birds.

All that remained was his heart, which lifted into the air, flying into the heavens to become the morning star. Forever after he was known as celestial Tlahuizcalpantecuhtli, the Lord of Dawn.

Quilaztli

Mexica (Nahua) tradition

Four goddesses
and woman combined,
her name is Quilaztli,
mighty, divine.
She can be a snake,
an eagle too.

She can be a star
or plants for food.
Precious bones
she knew to grind,
and then she shaped
all humankind.

When the Mexica set off on their pilgrimage from Aztlan to the place of the navel of the moon, which would be called Mexico Tenochtitlan, several portentous events occurred that revealed the strength of their gods.

At the beginning of their journey, two brave warriors named Mixcohuatl and Xiuhnel made an expedition into the wilderness to hunt game and thus feed the hungry Mexica.

Hours went by with no success. At some point after noon, they saw an eagle perched on a large cactus.

Immediately, the warriors nocked their arrows. The eagle, perceiving this movement, spread its wings and showed off its precious plumage. Mixcohuatl and Xiuhnel realized that this was no common eagle. Its magical nature was revealed as it began to speak.

"Mexica! Stop! You are about to commit a serious offense. If you want to kill me, do it. Here is my chest. But in exchange, you will have to pay dearly someday."

The sound of its voice made their skin crawl. Still, nervous as they were, the warriors loosed their arrows. Neither struck the eagle, which remained perched on the cactus, framed by the blooms of its prickly pears, staring at the warriors. Off they hurried, their hearts squeezed by some strange sorrow.

The Mexica continued on their way and arrived in Chimalco, where they settled for some time.

In the fourth year of their stay, during one of their monthly assemblies, a very tall woman burst into the circle of men, her body decked out in the trappings of war.

"Injustice has taken over the Mexica heart," said the woman. "Two of you have wronged a powerful goddess. As long as this offense remains unforgiven, you will make little headway. The end of your pilgrimage might be delayed years or perhaps centuries."

Everyone was silent, looking at one another, until the woman warrior headed to where Mixcohuatl and Xiuhnel were sitting.

The two realized that the powerful presence standing before them was related to the eagle they had found on the cactus. Mixcohuatl steeled himself, standing to address the woman warrior.

"Who are you to break into the assembly of the Mexica? If you are a woman, why do you carry shield and macana? Why are you dressed in the trappings of war? If you are a goddess and by chance you once took the form of the eagle our arrows threatened, reveal to us how we can honor you and make the sacrifices necessary for you to forgive our offense."

The majestic warrior replied, "I am Quilaztli, she who provides food to the sea-ringed world, she who ground the precious bones so that humanity could be fashioned, and she who nourished Quetzalcoatl, giving him strength when he was a child, in the long dream before time began. I am she who gave to human beings the mecapal and the coa, necessary tools for farming. And yes, Mexica, I'm also the eagle you found on the cactus, in my guise as Cuauhcihuatl, Eagle Woman. I am that snake that sends the rains and makes the earth fertile, so also know me as Cihuacoatl, Snake Woman. And fear my inscrutable nature, for as I command growth and abundance, I can rain down destruction like an ancient star. Then my name is Tzitzimicihuatl, Hellish Woman, source of misfortunes."

As the goddess spread her cape of eagle feathers, an overwhelming silence seized the assembly of the Mexica. Everyone lowered their heads and closed their eyes, for they understood the majesty of their goddess and what each of her four names could mean.

When they opened their eyes again, Quilaztli had disappeared. An eagle flew over the circle of the Mexica nobility, in the intense blue sky of Chimalco.

Oak Tree

Oceti Sakowin (Sioux) tradition

White fire
from on high.
Lightning strikes;
we shake and cry.

It sees everything,
sets what it wants alight.
Mighty Thunder Being—
Rain is now his wife.

When the Sioux nations lived unmolested in the world of trees and lakes, there was a family consisting of mother, father, a son named Utahu—Oak—and a daughter named Magaju—Rain. The siblings loved each other very much, each aiding the other with their respective chores. If Magaju was to repair the tipi, Utahu held and cut the threads. If Utahu went to the river to fetch water, then Magaju helped him carry the load.

One day, an unknown girl arrived in the village where the family lived. She stood in the midst of the tipis, so lost and alone that Magaju took pity on her and invited her into their home. The girl said her name was Hokemi: her parents had left one afternoon, never to return. Finding herself abandoned, she had started walking until she reached that village.

For a few years, the family lived in complete harmony, happy to have a new member, especially as she proved hardworking, sweet and well disposed.

But as she grew up, Hokemi's behavior became strange. She

would leave the tipi during the night and return at dawn, without anyone noticing. She stopped speaking to Magaju and only reluctantly completed her chores.

Hokemi now looked at Utahu with different eyes, a restless gaze full of darkness. She'd fallen in love with her adoptive brother and felt jealous of Magaju because the bond of affection between the blood siblings grew stronger every day. The young woman felt left out of the circle of love.

Utahu now had a tipi of his own. Only Magaju entered from time to time to help him with housework and to light the fire. No one had said so expressly, but Hokemi knew that she did not have the same rights as Magaju to enter the tipi.

One night, Utahu jolted awake, feeling someone watching him. He saw the silhouette of a woman, her head covered by a blanket, standing at the entrance of his tipi. Within seconds, it had faded stealthily. The event repeated itself several nights in a row, until Utahu, eager to know who the woman who kept visiting him was, threw a bit of burning wood from the small fire that warmed his tent. The coal hit the stranger in the face, but she did not let her blanket slip. Instead, she backed out of the tipi without so much as a groan.

The next day, the young man felt guilty for having caused the mysterious woman harm. Instead of going hunting, he sat beneath the branches of an oak to reflect. He fell asleep in that pensive position, lost in strange dreams the rest of the day and all of the night. Utahu awakened and tried to get up, but he could not move. By some strange magic, a small oak sapling had grown right overnight, its slender trunk passing through his body without causing pain, but rooting him to the ground as if he were also a tree.

Meanwhile, his family was distraught, not knowing his whereabouts. When dawn came, Magaju looked for him in his tipi and found it empty. She knew something bad had happened. Then, waking Hokemi, who slept beside her, so they could both look for Utahu, she saw that the other girl's face had been burned. *For some reason*, she thought, *misfortunes never come singly*.

The whole community went to work looking for the young man, until the old healer, Pagla, found him under a large oak tree with a smaller oak inside anchoring him in place.

"Your son has been bewitched," Pagla said to the anguished parents and sister. "It is a strange magic against which my knowledge has no power. If he tries to extract the tree from his body, Utahu will surely die. We can only depend upon the compassion and wisdom of the Great Spirit. If he allowed this magic to happen, there must be a reason."

Magaju felt she would die of despair. Raising her hands to the sky, she shouted with all the force of her lungs.

"Great Spirit! I ask you to release my brother. Send someone or something to save him. I promise to surrender my being in return and marry whoever releases him, be he man or spirit, young or old, handsome or hideous."

Many days passed in which nobody saw Hokemi again. The girl had vanished and the family cried their double misfortune.

One afternoon, a strange man arrived in the village. He was very tall and handsome, his long black hair held with a band around his forehead. His form was limned by an unearthly glow. Pagla dropped to the ground when he beheld the stranger. Many members of the community gathered around, including the family of Utahu.

"Who is the young woman who promised to marry whoever releases her brother?" asked the man.

"I am," said Magaju, trembling, overwhelmed by his regal elegance and the light emanating from his flesh.

"Woman, the Great Spirit has answered you and sent me. I am Wakangli, the powerful lightning that sees everything that happens from heaven and can annihilate an entire nation with one fell stroke of its celestial light. I am one of the Wakinya, the Thunder Beings! My voice echoes in the ravines, bursting the rocks. The bravest warriors tremble when they hear me and see my forking light! They run to seek refuge as stunned little beasts. The girl you adopted as a sister, the orphan you introduced into your family, into the shelter of your tipi, was a witch. She bewitched your brother out of spite because she had fallen in love with him, but knew he would never feel the same toward her. But she has already paid for the harm she has done. I ran across her on my way to this village. She was heading west, to the land of witches. With a blast of fire, I turned her to ash. The wind has dispersed what remained of her. Now I will free your brother. But first tell me, daughter of the earth, will you marry me, as you promised?"

Magaju replied with a thin and trembling voice:

"Yes, I will, mighty Wakangli, today, if you release my brother."

The stranger put his hands on the tree that emerged from Utahu's body. It was immediately reduced to ashes. The young man was able to stand at last. He hugged his sister and his parents tightly.

At that moment, a cloud darkened the sun. Wakangli looked up at it and took Magaju's hand. When their palms touched, the young woman was surrounded by an aura of beautiful blue light.

The cloud came down slowly and, as the community looked on, it wrapped itself around the couple and began to rise again, with them inside, to the very heights of heaven.

Then Thunder rumbled with his powerful voice and, by the will of the Great Spirit, the wedding of Magaju and Wakangli—Rain and Lightning—took place in the sky.

Rimac

Andean tradition

Wise Rimac
was an oracle;
the future
he could view.

To the prince he spoke
great prophecies
and all of them
came true.

In the distant times when what is now Peru was ruled by the Incas, there was an extraordinary figurine. Unlike other statues of the gods—huacas, the name given also to temples and sacred places—this idol could speak and prophesy the future.

Thus the priests named him Rimac, meaning "he who speaks." Because his sanctuary is in a valley, the river took the name of the oracle. The Incan dialect of Quechua made Rimac "Limaq," and after the Spanish conquest, the word became "Lima" on foreign tongues, the future name of the capital of Peru.

Large pilgrimages were organized in those remote years to ask Rimac if crops would be abundant, if the Incas would subdue their enemies, if an earthquake was near and what would be the best way to survive natural disasters.

One day, Prince Pachacutec, divine son of the great Inca

Viracocha, came to consult Rimac. He was confused about his future. Though his father had not designated him as successor, the prince wanted to give shape to the ideas that were swirling in his head concerning the Kingdom of Cuzco, realm of the Incas.

So Pachacutec arrived at the temple, and the priests went out to receive him, aware of the importance of the individual who had asked to consult Rimac.

The prince was taken to the chamber where the statue shone. Covered with gold, crowned with a diadem, arms outstretched with open palms as if to bestow wondrous gifts, Rimac gazed at the man kneeling at his feet and his pupils lit up.

"Your heart is restless, Pachacutec," said the huaca, and a shiver went up the prince's spine as sacred terror seized him.

Steeling himself, Pachacutec replied:

"That's right, wise Rimac. I fear that my father will not name me heir to the throne of Cuzco."

"Do you seek power for power's sake alone?" asked the huaca. "Know that ambition can make you lose your sanity."

"No. I want to succeed my father in order to make the kingdom greater. I have dreams in which gods visit me and show me the changes that must come. But I'm confused, so I've come to consult you."

"What do you want to know?"

"Whether it is prudent to attack the Chancas, our rivals for supremacy in these lands."

"The Chancas are my dear children," said Rimac. "They founded my sanctuary and make sacrifices that power my huaca."

Pachacutec was at a loss. He felt that he had asked the wrong question and offended the god.

"However," Rimac continued, "the ideas that swirl in your

mind are also mine, these plans you have to make yourself worthy of succeeding Viracocha. But I do not mean the destruction of the Chancas, who will not perish, but will live a longer life through their fusion with your people."

Rimac kept a brief silence. Pachacutec looked anxiously at his face. Finally, the god pronounced one word:

"Tahuantinsuyo."

"My lord, what do you mean by saying 'four regions'?"

"That you are destined to gather the earth. That you will win in your campaign against the Chancas and that your father Viracocha will name you his heir. You will not reign over Cuzco alone, but above all the world. Your kingdom will be called Tahuantinsuyo. It will know no boundaries while it lasts."

Pachacutec left the sanctuary of Rimac, his heart burning at the majesty of his dream.

Everything happened as the prophetic huaca had said: Rimac defeated the bellicose Chancas and Viracocha named him his heir.

Under the command of this visionary prince, who would be called "Inca Who Changes the Direction of Earth," the nations were united, and the great empire of Tahuantinsuyo was born.

Sedna

Inuit tradition

Sedna lives in the North,
that ice country fair.
Stars of frost
bejewel her hair.

Queen of the waves,
protector of fishermen.
No sea creature stirs
without her assent.

Sedna lived with her widowed father in the land of shining ice. The beauty of the young woman had attracted fishermen and travelers, who longed to marry her. But she rejected them all, not wanting to abandon her father, who depended on her for food, conversation and company.

One day a boat glided to a stop near their home. It was piloted by a man decked out in blue skins.

Sedna saw him arrive while pulling small fish from the ice to feed her father. The man disembarked and fixed his gaze on Sedna. She stood up slowly, entranced at the sight of the stranger, her heart beating when he extended his hand. Without hesitation, Sedna laced her fingers in his, abandoning the fish and all concern for her father to board the boat of that unknown man.

For weeks, her old father grieved the disappearance of his daughter. Each afternoon, he visited the places where she used to fish, fixing his eyes on the sea-horizon. *The gods have taken her*, he thought. *She was too beautiful for this land of ice.*

One of those afternoons, the father heard a sad lament. It came from the sea, from far offshore, a song of infinite misfortune or tortured loneliness. The father thought he recognized his daughter's voice.

His heart had not deceived him. It was indeed Sedna who intoned that mournful chant in the distance.

The man who had taken her over the icy waters was a sorcerer. He had confined her for weeks, forcing her to perform arduous tasks. Her hands were chapped and red, her eyes blurry. She missed her father very much, but she had lost hope of regaining her freedom.

The old man steeled himself to follow the echoes of that lament and find his daughter. He boarded his old kayak, daring danger upon the gray waters of the open sea.

Fatherly love guided him in the darkness of the night, and he reached the icy fortress where the sorcerer lived. Sedna crouched by the shore, dressed in tatters, shivering with cold. The sorcerer had ordered her to wash a hundred skins in the frigid waters. Seeing her father, the young woman stood, joy and relief on her features. Then she ran with all her strength and boarded the kayak.

Father and daughter had already left the cruel fortress behind them when the sorcerer, roaring with rage, wielded his magical arts. He stirred the sea into a merciless maelstrom, thrusting wave after wave toward his escaping prisoner. A swirl of salt and fear enveloped the kayak, and Sedna fell into the water.

Struggling to keep her head above water, Sedna managed to swim to the kayak and cling to the gunwale. But her father, driven mad by terror and black magic, desperate to survive what had to be the wrath of the very gods, seized his ax.

Though his daughter begged him to stop, the old man hacked off her fingers. Her hands slipped from the kayak, and Sedna sank screaming beneath the waves.

In his mind, her father believed the sea was trying to claim her. Its divine power was too great for him to oppose.

When the young woman's fingers touched the water, they became fish and seals and walruses and whales . . . and all other creatures that inhabit the sea.

At once, the ocean calmed its fury, becoming a tranquil mirror reflecting the endless gray sky. Sedna sank into the depths and, fathoms down, regained her dazzling beauty. She became the goddess of the sea, invoked by sailors and fishermen alike.

As ages passed, Sedna learned to love again. Mighty Qailertetang, goddess of the weather, joined her there in the heart of the sea. Two-spirit shamans attend them, performing the rites that keep the goddesses content. Together, Sedna and her beloved Qailertetang protect both hunter and prey, sustaining life in the cold and beautiful land of the Inuit people.

Sibo

Cabecar and Bribri tradition

In that pebble,
free from our hate,
hidden from all,
Sibo awaits.

Humblest of men,
creator incarnate;
he makes us better,
he changes our fates.

The Bribri and Cabecar people of Costa Rica know Sibo well, creator god, originator of the universe. After making the land and putting humans upon it, he chose to be born again, small and defenseless, like any mortal child.

He was floating in a river, wrapped in a thin and translucent skin, when found by the mother of Sorkula, a powerful shaman who ruled the land, intimidating all. Although he possessed great knowledge, he never used it to cure diseases and reverse misfortunes, but to dominate others and profit from them.

Sorkula was resting in his hammock when his mother placed the newborn in his hands, saying, "This is your little brother. You must protect him."

Sorkula looked closely at the baby, then shook his head, laying him on the floor.

"That's no brother of mine. You do wrong attempting to deceive me, Mother. You will see in time."

Sibo was raised by Sorkula's parents. When he grew into a young man, he told people who he really was, how he had created the world in his previous life, and how he had brought land from the farthest regions of the world to give them the very best.

At first people listened to him carefully, asking him to tell them stories of those ancient times, but one day, one man whispered to another, "Sibo was born to kill us. That is why he's come. To kill us. To wipe everyone from the face of the earth."

The rumor passed from mouth to mouth until all the people were convinced their destruction was at hand.

Sorkula, who had been waiting for the right moment to get rid of Sibo, gathered the people in the square and told them, "That charlatan claims to be Sibo, but he really isn't. He has been preaching falsehoods for years. His true goal is to kill us all. Before that happens, we must act first. Seize Sibo and kill him!"

Rallied by his words, the men went in a mob to look for Sibo, who was walking absently along the riverbank. He did not resist as they dragged him to a tree and tied him up, planning to kill him the next day.

First, of course, they wanted to celebrate. Thus were they delayed: they all drank potent chicha and got drunk. It was not until the fourth day that they returned to finish Sibo off.

But the ropes were lying on the ground at the foot of the tree. Sibo had escaped!

As he could transform himself into what he wanted, Sibo had become a pebble. Rolling, he reached the feet of Sorkula. The wizard knew immediately who the timid stone was. He pronounced magic words that made Sibo return to human form.

Without wasting time, Sorkula lifted his bow and shot an arrow at Sibo that pierced his flesh. He shot a second, a third and a fourth . . . but Sibo could not die.

Then it was Sibo's turn. He sent three arrows flying. Sorkula stopped them with his magic. The fourth, however, ripped through the wizard's heart. He fell instantly dead.

With slow, deliberate steps, Sibo walked through the town. Everyone he encountered, he shot with an arrow. Each fell dead, but then Sibo revived and remade them, forging a new head, molding their heart, reweaving their hair.

So he did with every man, woman, and child. One by one he made them better than they were.

That was why he had come to earth again.

Tamoanchan

Nahua tradition

It's like a garden
with heavenly blooms;
it's like a star
that shines through the gloom.
Within it, a tree
burgeons with hope

though one of its boughs
sundered and broke.
The Nahuas proclaim,
"To live is to dream."
We awaken at last
in Tamoanchan.

Many years ago, so many that no one could count them, our grandfathers and grandmothers—dressed in white, their hair tied back—landed on the northern beaches, in Panutla, the Place of Crossing.

Our grandparents continued on their way, always guided by wise ones who possessed the ancient books. They arrived at a place they liked very much. They named it Tamoanchan: "we are looking for our home."

Warm breezes, golden sun, turquoise birds and jade-green fish, wind whispering through the boughs of the trees, dreamy sunrises and sunsets in which unimaginable colors braided together, clear water and the eternal youth of natural things.

There, Lord Quetzalcoatl had brought the precious bones, once he had rescued them from the land of the dead after blowing the conch. There Quilaztli had ground them to flour in order to fashion humanity with love and hope. There the lovely Xochiquetzal had lived with her countless flowers. In peace in that land had coexisted the Hummingbird of the South, the Cloud Serpent, and the Obsidian Butterfly. Tlaloc, Lord of Storms, and his wife the Divine Lady of the Jade Skirt had spent long millennia in that paradise.

"Tamoanchan encompasses all of this," the wise ones read aloud from their books, teaching our grandmothers and grandfathers. From the books they heard the words of the supreme god, that dual force that created itself. Tloqueh Nahuaqueh, Lord of the Near and the Nigh. Ipalnemohuani, Giver of Life.

One day that god told them to leave again, to set off on the journey once more, taking the black and red ink of the sacred books. But not everyone would depart. Only the tlamatinimeh, the wisest of sages, would travel to the East, on a new journey to the place of origin, while the other grandfathers and grandmothers, already properly instructed, would remain in Tamoanchan.

Among them were Oxomoco and Cipactonal, the very first humans, ancestors of us all, who held hands and exclaimed:

"There will be light! It will dawn again! But how will people live? How will they establish themselves? In what direction should they walk? What goals should they pursue? What, beloved gods, will be their measuring stick?"

At that moment, a deafening noise echoed all around. The most beautiful tree in Tamoanchan had split in two. Its branches were torn and blood flowed from them. Most of its flowers, which turned anyone who touched them into a faithful lover, now lay scattered on the ground, bloodied.

Oxomoco and Cipactonal looked at the broken tree and then at each other. Oxomoco spoke first.

"Tamoanchan is now the place of detachment. The wise ones departed and took the books, but they left us love, blood and memory."

And Cipactonal said, in his florid tongue, "What place could we go where death does not exist? Not forever on earth: just a moment we live."

Oxomoco took from the tree an immaculate flower, a bloom that did not bleed. Breathing in its delicate aroma, she spoke words of encouragement:

"Cheer up, my heart. Listen to the song of the birds, wonder at the beauty of a flower. Only in you will they not cease. Only within you will they never wilt. Only within you will Tamoanchan forever endure."

Tlalocan

Nahua tradition

Goggles of jade
cover his eyes,
glittering gaze,
thunderbolt eyebrows.

He rules Tlalocan,
pouring down gifts:
rain and grass,
flowery boughs.

Once, a boy named Michin was playing on the lakeshore. His mother wasn't worried. Her son was an excellent swimmer who could hold his breath underwater as he searched for shiny pebbles, so she let him have his fun. Michin liked to stare at the various hues of blue and green layered within the lake, his eyes delighting in the swaths of blue layered in the water and following on its surface dashing shadows of the clouds and the dance of the reflected boughs.

That afternoon, two fantastic animals drew near. One was an ahuizotl, an otter-like creature with a fifth hand at the end of its tail; the other an ateponaztli, a black-headed water bird with yellowish plumage.

Ahuizotl was the first to speak:

"Boy, you have been coming to our lake for many days."

"It's not that we don't like it; on the contrary," Ateponaztli clarified.

"And to prove it," said Ahuizotl, "we want to extend to you an invitation."

"To where?" asked the boy.

"To the most beautiful place in the cosmos," Ateponaztli replied.

"Why is it the most beautiful place?" asked Michin.

"Because there are seeds and honey of every type," Ahuizotl explained.

"And fruits and tortillas, plus butterflies and frogs that you never get tired of playing with," Ateponaztli added.

"How do I reach that place?" The boy was interested.

"Follow us!" the two fantastic animals said in unison, and they plunged into the lake.

The boy had no idea that Ahuizotl and Ateponaztli are treacherous creatures. They roam lakes and rivers to attract people and make them drown. That's their role in the order of things: take the drowned to Tlalocan to appear before those great sovereigns of the waters, Tlaloc and Chalchiuhtlicue, so that their souls become tlaloques and help bring rain to everyone.

But what Ahuizotl and Ateponaztli did not know was that Michin was a very good swimmer and diver. As a result, they were very surprised when they reached the bottom of the lake and saw Michin arrive with hardly an effort, holding his breath, his eyes wide open.

As the tricky creatures were out of air, they had no choice but to open the magic portal, and all three shot through it at the same time.

Ahuizotl slammed the door behind them so that water wouldn't rush through. On the other side Michin found he could breathe just fine. All around them stretched a sunny garden.

As soon as he could speak, Ahuizotl demanded, "How did you do it?"

"Do what?" asked Michin.

"You were supposed to drown!" shouted Ateponaztli.

Before Michin could respond, wonderful music reverberated through the air, setting the boughs to sway and the leaves to shake.

"Lord Tlaloc!" said Ahuizotl and Ateponaztli at the same time.

The two threw themselves to the ground, bowing their heads. Michin stood and stared at the most beautiful being he had ever seen. Blue goggles encircled his eyes and glinted in the sunlight; his eyebrows were golden thunderbolts. His face was human, but with the features of a jaguar, fangs the color of jade jutting from his mouth.

Michin was overwhelmed with astonishment. Before him stood Lord Tlaloc, master of water, lightning, storms, the origin of all life on earth, perhaps the greatest of the gods.

"Child of the earth," said Lord Tlaloc, "how did you get here with your living body? You must be someone very special. Tell me first your name and then your reasons. You have my full attention."

"Lord Tlaloc, my name is Michin. I have arrived here following two fantastic animals that told me this is the most beautiful place in the cosmos," the boy replied. Then he added, "I am a good swimmer and a bit of a diver, so I did not hesitate to follow them."

"Michin means 'fish,'" murmured Lord Tlaloc. "Naming you thus, your parents gave you a valuable gift. And now that you are here, I recognize the will of the Lord of the Near and the Nigh, he who invents himself. Though you may be a living boy, I shall show you Tlalocan. Come, follow me."

Ahuizotl and Ateponaztli decided to withdraw discreetly in case Lord Tlaloc should want to rebuke them for not doing their job well. Michin walked behind the majestic blue presence, and they soon arrived at a waterfall where a lady stood waiting, dressed in a beautiful green huipil skirt. The boy marveled, because the huipil was not cloth, but water.

"She is my wife, Chalchiuhtlicue," said Lord Tlaloc.

As they continued their walk, Michin saw many people dressed in bright colors conversing, playing ball, chasing butterflies and painting in books of amate paper. There were many crystalline rivers where smiling children splashed joyfully in the water, playing with delightful frogs that enjoyed the game as much as the humans.

"This is my paradise," said Lord Tlaloc, "a refuge for the souls of all who die by water or touched by lightning, or who have suffered from leprosy and dropsy, whose disabilities came at birth or through accident. It sits on the eastern edge of the cosmos. All who behold it swear it is the most beautiful realm of all. Tell me, Michin: would you like to stay here? You would become an assistant to my wife, Chalchiuhtlicue, and me, helping us bring the water to the world."

Michin felt so happy in the depths of Tlalocan that for a moment he considered accepting Lord Tlaloc's proposal. But then he thought of his mother and father, his friends and his elderly teacher. He suddenly wished with all his might to see them again.

"Ah. You have answered me," said Lord Tlaloc, looking into the boy's heart. "Then return, Michin. Take care of your world. Teach everyone that there is no wealth or precious jewel that compares with the value of water."

Uirapuru

Guarani tradition

Do you know
that Uirapuru
is the faithful bird
of the sky so blue?
She weeps for him,
does sweet Arami,
because their love
can never be.
So there in the jungle
forever he sings
both night and day
his melody.

An arrow had pierced the heart of Uirapuru, the bravest warrior of the Amazon, one covered with the deadliest of poisons. The pain it caused would not let him live; it took away his breath and his desire to eat, tormenting him relentlessly.

The arrow that had wounded him had not been loosed from the bow of another warrior, nor had it flown from some hunter who missed the mark when aiming at the fierce jaguar.

No, it was the arrow of love, and the passion he felt was its poison.

Wretched Uirapuru! He had fallen in love with the wife of the cacique of his tribe, the beautiful Arami, bright as the morning skies. She felt the same, but their love could not be. It was forbidden by the laws of men. If the chief discovered the truth, both would be sentenced to death.

Uirapuru suffered so much that the god Tupa, who is moved by the plight of human beings, spoke to him from the soft mist of dawn in that enchanted land.

"Do you feel love, Uirapuru? Well done. The world looks very different to those in love, bathed with a new light. Life extends like the wings of a bird, and the soul creates exquisite melodies."

"I'm sure it's as you say, but I'm suffering terribly," said Uirapuru. "I will never be able to touch my beloved, or listen enraptured to her voice, or gaze upon her beautiful face for hours, or cross the jungle of youth by her side until we reach old age, as is my wish, Tupa."

"I know," said the god. "I want to help you, Uirapuru. I cannot change the situation. Arami will continue as the wife of the cacique, and you will continue to love her without hope. But I can take away the bitter pain."

"How?" asked Uirapuru.

"By transforming you into a bird. That way you can visit your beloved every day, listen to her voice, and gaze upon her beautiful face. And you can also sing to her the exquisite melody of your enamored soul."

So Tupa did, and the pain disappeared from Uirapuru's heart. Now a bird, he arrived every morning at Arami's house. There he stayed long hours, singing a song so beautiful that all who heard it fell silent at once to better listen. Even the other birds stopped their trilling.

The song fell upon the ears of the cacique, and that leader decided he must have the bird that sang it for himself. He ordered his men to build a cage and trap Uirapuru inside it.

How fiercely the tiny bird fought against the hands of his captors! With what cunning and agility did he defend his freedom! Uirapuru escaped, but not before throwing a melancholy look at Arami, who was crying inconsolably, and then heading for the jungle. There he took refuge, in the most intricate, the most hidden depths, where no one could ever find him.

Since then, the bird sings deep in the Amazon jungle. When passing travelers happen to hear his voice, they can consider themselves lucky.

They have heard the song of love, forever intoned for no one yet for all, by the faithful Uirapuru.

Universe

Mexica (Nahua) tradition

Below, the levels
number nine.
Thirteen heavens
above us rise.

Quetzalcoatl
wants to converse—
he'll guide you through
the universe.

Look, Quetzalli," the girl's mother said one day when she took her to see the Great Temple in the sacred precinct of Tenochtitlan, city of the Mexica. "Where the two shrines of our lord Huitzilopochtli and our lord Tlaloc meet? That is the center of the universe. We cannot see clearly, because we are simple people, but the priests and the great lord Moctezuma perceive, from that point, the thirteen heavens above and the nine levels of Mictlan, land of the dead, below."

They returned home, alternating between walking and canoe rides, as half the streets of Tenochtitlan were canals.

Quetzalli kept quiet all day, thinking about what her mother had said. When evening fell, she went out to the patio and breathed in the smell of the wet earth, as it had rained a little. A bright spot in the sky caught her attention, filling her with wonder. It was the evening star! Quetzalli's mother had told her that glittering light was one of the forms that Lord Quetzalcoatl had taken after leaving the great city of Tollan, promising to return.

The spot got brighter and brighter. Quetzalli realized it was growing in size, approaching her! The light became so intense that she closed her eyes. When she opened them again, before her stood the most beautiful being she had ever seen.

He was a tall young man with strange silver hair. He wore a sectioned shell pendant on his chest. The wind jewel.

"Like a star," thought Quetzalli.

"That I am, among other things," said the young man. "You have been thinking of me, so I decided to leave heaven and ask you to accompany me on a trip that you will never forget."

"Who are you?" asked Quetzalli.

"I have many names. They call me the Divine Twin and the Feathered Serpent. Some know me as the Lord of the House of Dawn, my longest name." The young man smiled.

"You are Quetzalcoatl!" exclaimed the girl.

"That's right, and your name is like the precious bird that gives me mine," said the young man. "Will you come with me then? We don't have much time, but I want to show you the universe."

Quetzalli nodded, and Quetzalcoatl took her hand. In the blink of an eye they were transported to the Great Temple she had visited that morning with her mother. She and the lord of creation stood right in the spot where the temples of the two great gods come together.

This time, Quetzalli could clearly see a kind of vertical tunnel with translucent walls that rose to the sky and sank into the earth. The girl saw that along its length rose and fell animals and humans of great beauty and luminous bodies: jaguars and eagles, noble lords and ladies wearing feathers and precious jades.

"First we will go to the underworld," Quetzalcoatl said, "all the way to the heart of Mictlan."

Without releasing Quetzalli's hand, he drew her into the tunnel. They began, not to fall, but to descend gently, like the feather of a bird drifting down from the sky.

And Quetzalli saw and passed through the nine levels of the underworld. She witnessed the purifying trials the souls of the dead must overcome. The river that one must cross accompanied by a xoloitzcuintle dog. The mountains that separate to slam together again. A mountain bristling with obsidian knives. A snow-covered wasteland. A wasteland where the wind shakes people as if they were flags. The path where arrows rain. The dark deserts where wild beasts threaten to devour one's heart. The river of dark waters. And finally nine thrashing rivers, weaving together. Although they were all terrible places, Quetzalli was not afraid because Quetzalcoatl was by her side.

"Prepare yourself, because now we will visit the heavens," said the god.

Quetzalcoatl blew a conch, and a harmonious sound trumpeted forth. A wind rose that lifted them back through the tunnel. In a few seconds, they were upon the temple once more. Surprised, Quetzalli suddenly spread her arms. She now had wings and could fly on her own! Lifting herself upward, she saw the great city of Tenochtitlan spread out below her, a jewel surrounded by turquoise rings. She breathed the purest of air as she rose above the snowy peaks of the Iztaccihuatl and Popocatepetl volcanoes.

Suddenly it became dark. Quetzalli saw and passed through the thirteen levels of heaven. The heaven of the moon, where a silver lady with bells on her face combed her long hair and braided it with feathers and shells. The heaven where the stars move, containing the Milky Way and the constellations. The heaven of the sun and another nearby containing its path across the sky. She saw the realm of comets and the heaven that belongs to Tezcatlipoca, lord of darkness. She saw the heaven of Huitzilopochtli, where he and his warriors protect the rising sun.

Quetzalli was counting the heavens as she flew through them. She knew that she had reached the eighth when her wings got wet, for it was the realm of storms. Then followed the heaven where light moves, source of eclipses. A heaven of the eastern sky, tinged with yellow. A heaven of the western sky, scarlet red, where heat reigns and the god of fire dwells.

"We have reached my abode," Quetzalcoatl said as they reached the twelfth heaven. "This is my original home, where I have lived since the beginning of the world with my brothers, Tezcatlipoca, lord of the North; Xipe Totec, lord of the East; and Huitzilopochtli, the great Hummingbird of the South. The West belongs to me. That is why my temples on earth always direct their façades to this cardinal point."

Quetzalli thought she would never tire of looking at the beautiful abodes of the brother gods: four temples of carved stone inlaid with turquoise, arranged around a massive plaza cobbled with jade.

"Now, Quetzalli," said the god, "all that is left is the thirteenth heaven. But we will not enter it because it is the most sacred place of all, the place of origin from which everything arises and to which everything eventually returns: my being, yours, everyone's. It is Omeyocan, the Place of Duality, where the Supreme Lord and Lady live, Ometeuctli and Omecihuatl, God and Goddess. They are halves of a whole, Ometeotl, Two That Are One, One That Is All, the amazing universe itself."

Blue Deer

Wixarika (Huichol) tradition

"I want to arrive,"
the Blue Deer cried.
"A star awaits me
in the distant sky."
Run through the sea,
run toward the meadows;
don't let the hunters
shoot you with arrows.
But if they reach you,
Brother Blue Deer,
embrace your visions
free from all fear.

When everything was sea and beings inhabited it, the waves whispered in the ear of our elder brother Kauyumari, the Blue Deer:

"It's time to leave. The stars await."

The Blue Deer trembled with excitement, a ray of joy shooting through his body. He ran lightly across the coral fields and reached the foam meadows.

The waves held hands and surrounded the five hunters, men with dark eyes and beautiful skin the color of clay, who lived in the sea beside the ancestors and the wolves. Joining their voices, the waves gave their command:

"It's time for you to depart. The Blue Deer runs through the fields, and your duty is to hunt him. The stars are waiting."

The five hunters took up their bows and arrows and without hesitation rushed from the depths of the sea to the surface.

The ancestors received the same command from the waves. They caressed the fur of their wolves with dreamy eyes, preparing to leave the sea at once and walk upon the land, also following the tracks of the Blue Deer.

With them went young Morning Star, armed with his brave and pure arrows.

With them went the One-Eyed Child of the Moon, carrying arrows with feathered tips and a small basket.

The road never ended. But then young Morning Star took one of his arrows, pulled back his bowstring, and shot toward a solitary rock. The rock burst into flames! Then Morning Star smiled, joining with the fire. His glow lit the way for the five hunters, the ancestors, the wolves and the One-Eyed Child of the Moon. Everyone could clearly make out the prints of the Blue Deer.

They soon discovered a gigantic flower. Its petals swayed back and forth like a huge nodding head. Its iridescent colors were so beautiful that no one could stop staring. The five hunters slowed their hurried pace when they saw it. If they could only caress those soft petals, breathe in that scent, just for a moment, a fleeting instant, before finally catching Blue Deer . . .

"It's the kieri. The mad herb," the ancestors whispered. "It is true that it reveals, but it also devours. Only one of us can taste it. Only one of us can become a healer, a mara'akame, without losing their mind. Who will it be?"

And the ancestors looked at one another in silence, still walking after Blue Deer.

The earth, little by little, became dry. The five hunters, the ancestors, the wolves and the One-Eyed Child of the Moon had come to the desert. Their legs were weak, their throats parched. They grew thirsty. One of the ancestors felt the inner need to become water. She fell to her knees on the dry ground, and from within her chest burst a serpent that became rain, falling water, clear as thought. There she remained as a spring to purify the road. Forever she was known as Tatei Matinieri, one of our mothers, the snake of western rain.

"There's the Blue Deer!" shouted the five hunters.

"The stars await me," the Blue Deer said in his dream tongue.

He ran faster, and the five hunters did the same. The Blue Deer's path led his pursuers to Wirikuta, to the Hill of Dawn, where everything was about to happen forever.

The Blue Deer folded his legs and offered his life to the five hunters. The first bolt flew. And the second. The third, the fourth, the fifth.

The Blue Deer had reached its destination: a meadow, a forest, a place of delight, a field of love.

The five hunters, forming a circle of respectful silence, ate Blue Deer's heart, which had flowered into the hikuri plant.

At that same moment, on the Hill of Dawn, the One-Eyed Child of the Moon was reborn as the sun.

Everything lit up. The mountains, the earth, the sky—all of it shone. The brightest colors unfolded before the eyes of the ancestors and their wolves, which were already fading into dream.

Abandoned on the ground were the feather-tipped arrows and basket of the One-Eyed Child of the Moon.

They saw the sun in the sky. And in the sun they saw a bright, clear and perfect face. So they painted their faces with yellow circles and sang without tiring.

For in Wirikuta, the ancestors had reached the end of their path from the sea. They had witnessed the creation of the sun. And they had obtained the greatest gift—nierika, the ability to see the world through the beautiful eyes of the Blue Deer.

Viracocha

Andean tradition

Viracocha gave names
to every nation.
Landscapes and people
were his creation.
He gave us the stars,
taught us how to behave.

His robes were white,
and he left on the waves.
He promised that one day
he would return.
May he come back soon
from his long sojourn!

When Viracocha created the world, he did not give sun to the day, nor stars or moon to the night. Instead, he decided to populate it. To that end, he sketched out a race of giants on huge stones. Upon comparing them to himself, he realized it would be preferable to fashion humanity with his own dimensions. He then created people in his own likeness. That first generation lived in darkness.

He instructed them to live according to reasonable rules and precepts, without violating nature or themselves, without vices, quarrels or envies. People obeyed for a time until injustice wormed its way into their midst. Viracocha punished them, turning them into stones. Many were pulverized and others were swallowed by the sea. The god decided the world should change course. So he turned his back on that first creation, sending a flood that ended it all.

Viracocha indeed destroyed everyone, except three men, whom he kept as assistants in carrying out his second creation. Once the earth had dried up, Viracocha and his servants went to an island in the middle of a lagoon called Titicaca. From there he threw stars into the sky, saying to himself that his new world should be luminous: the sun for the day, the moon and stars for the night. Oddly enough, the moon shone brighter than the sun. Full of jealous rage, the sun threw ashes onto the face of the moon, dulling his light.

One of Viracocha's assistants, Taguapacac, rebelled against him and refused to comply with his orders. So Viracocha sent the other two to tie him up and set him adrift on a raft in the middle of the lagoon. As they complied, Taguapacac shouted curses against Viracocha and swore that he would return to exact revenge. The raft was dragged by a current to the edge of a waterfall. The disobedient servant disappeared over that raging edge.

Viracocha and his assistants abandoned the island and the lagoon, leaving behind one of the first huacas. They walked without tiring until they arrived in Tiahuanaco, where Viracocha was seized by a frenzy of creation and upon huge slabs sketched all the nations he planned to create. He drew mountains, valleys and villages and said their names, instructing his assistants to commit them to memory.

So they did, and Viracocha instructed them to go off walking and shouting the names they had learned. One of the assistants headed toward the South Sea, the other to the Andes, while Viracocha walked and shouted names in the central lands. In this way, the three went creating the landscapes of what is now Peru and the people that would inhabit them.

Viracocha was of medium height and light brown complexion,

with long hair that he held back with a band around his forehead. He always wore white and bore a staff in one hand, a book in the other. It was a strange sight for humanity, because the sort of book he carried was unknown then in the Tahuantinsuyo. In a deliberate and clear voice, Viracocha shared his teachings, making valleys resonate with the words he intoned in the Quechua language.

Thus he walked for centuries among the people until, accompanied by his two faithful assistants, he reached the ends of Peruvian lands. Then he announced to the peoples he had created that it was time for him to leave.

"Someday," he said, "there will come men like me, claiming to be Viracocha. You should not believe them. It will not be true. When I return, believe me, I will give clear signals. Then the world will change course once again."

Viracocha fell silent and with his two assistants went down to the sea. People at the shoreline saw them walking upon the waves, never sinking. Their white robes shone in the sun until they were lost on the horizon.

Gichi-manidoo

Ojibwe tradition

In the Great Lakes,
their sands like the moon,
a mother bear sleeps,
turned into a dune.
She dreams of her children,
two brave little cubs;
she lost them one night,
in spite of her love.

Gichi-manidoo
had pity at last,
transforming her pain
into glittering sand.
Dream, Mother Bear,
a joy without measure—
you and your cubs,
together forever.

Flames devoured the tallest trees and the air soon became unbreathable.

The bear knew the only escape, the only way to save her two cubs, was to leave the burning forest and defy the icy waters of the Great Lakes.

She was a good swimmer. She would do all she could to keep her cubs afloat. There was no time to find another path out of the destruction. Flames danced in time to the hiss and crackle of wood as it collapsed, overcome by inexorable fire.

The bear guided her two little ones to the lake. Though the smoke roiled thicker and thicker, her instinct, more than her eyes, saw the farther shore. Between the fire and safety, the expanse of water. Between looming death and possible life, desperate effort.

The bear pushed her cubs into the water and immediately dove in after them. They swam for a few long minutes during which fog or smoke or both grew so dense that the mother could not distinguish the heads and snouts of her little ones, who kept paddling as hard as they could with paws gone numb with heat and cold.

The mother spotted the safe farther shore and managed to reach it. Trusting that her cubs would soon arrive at her side, she sank her paws in the sand and climbed to the top of the dune. There, she stared toward the smoke-covered water and waited.

Long days passed with their long nights. The hopeful mother bear never moved from her hopeless dune. Her eyes strained at the horizon, her nose alert to the scent of the warm fur, the unmistakable breath of her children.

Motionless on top of the dune, in the midst of the beautiful and merciless landscape of the Great Lakes, pain eating at her heart, not feeling hunger or thirst, the mother waited.

Gichi-manidoo—the Great Spirit, the Great Mystery, who has no face, no eyes, no hands, but can know and see and touch everything, because he created it—took pity on the mother bear. Seeing her suffer, he draped her with the softest blanket of moon-silvered sand so that her soul could rejoin those of her cubs.

And in the place where they had drowned, fighting for their lives in frigid waters, Gichi-manidoo made two islands surge from the lake.

Sleeping Bear Dunes, the people of the Great Lakes call the tomb of the mother bear. And somewhere within the Great Mystery, which is called Gichi-manidoo, the cubs play forever, safe from death and fire.

Waleker

Wayuu tradition

Waleker, Spider,
what do you weave?
Flowers and life?
A web in the leaves?
The Wayuu people
hold you dear

because your threads
weave light and clear.
Irunnu still thinks
and dreams of you.
Never forget
that, young Wayuu.

One morning, a young man went hunting in the jungle. Handsome and athletic, the hunter lived with his three sisters in a village on the peninsula of Guajira, land of the Wayuu people. His name was Irunnu—Falling Star.

He had been walking for a short time, when under a tree he found a girl with matted hair and dirty clothes, playing with a row of ants. Surprised to see a little girl alone in the jungle, he asked her name and where her parents were.

"My name is Waleker," said the girl. "My parents are dead. I have no one in the world."

Irunnu took pity on the girl and decided to take her to live at his home. When they saw his new charge, his three sisters balked. They were unwilling to live with such a dirty and disagreeable little brat. A tear fell from Waleker's eyes as she turned to look questioningly at Irunnu, who replied to his sisters with brusque authority.

"I am not asking for permission, but giving an order. Waleker will live with us."

"We don't have enough food," said one of the women.

"I will feed her with the game that I hunt," Irunnu replied.

"And I promise to help with all the housework," Waleker said in a voice so soft that Irunnu's sisters did not hear it. Reluctantly, they let her into the house.

While the women had no choice but to accept her presence, they continually showed their contempt for the girl. They gave her the toughest tasks only to criticize her work, accusing her of being lazy, dirty and foul smelling. They would not feed her, so she had to wait, playing with the ants, for Irunnu to arrive at the end of the day. Then he, with a smile, would share his own food with her.

A few weeks after Waleker arrived at the house of Irunnu and his sisters, woven fabrics with the most beautiful designs began to appear. First, the siblings discovered a dazzling hammock stretched wall to wall. When they tried it, they discovered it could produce wonderful dreams for any who slept in it. Those who sat on it spoke with eloquent and charming words.

Then, four Wayuu backpacks appeared, one for each family member. Finally, they awoke to find the floor covered with a carpet so beautiful and bright that it gave the siblings' home an enchanted atmosphere.

None knew where the beautiful fabrics had come from. When Waleker was asked if she had seen anything out of the ordinary, she shrugged and continued playing with the ants.

Irunnu was determined to solve the mystery. One day he snuck home at a different hour than usual. In the corner where Waleker usually waited for him, he saw a beautiful young woman wearing richly embroidered clothes, working a simple loom, hands flashing between warp and weft. From her mouth came bright threads with which she wove her fabric.

Irunnu approached her. Attracted by her beauty, he felt an urge to embrace her. The young woman, sensing his presence and closeness, gave a shout and ran out of the house.

Irunnu followed her, but she ran so fast he couldn't reach her. In his pursuit, Irunnu left his village behind and entered the jungle. It was already night when the maiden finally stopped her running. Irunnu realized that they had reached the place where he had first found Waleker playing with the ants.

The beautiful stranger stood at the foot of that same tree.

"Who you are?" Irunnu whispered, approaching very slowly so as not to scare her.

"I am Waleker, the Spider. I came to this land to teach the Wayuu the art of weaving. I thank you for taking me in, but I sense your feelings. Know this, Irunnu: I can't love you. I'm not human."

"Marry me, beautiful Waleker!" the young man cried. "For you I am willing to do everything, to stop being human and become what you want."

"It's not possible, sweet Irunnu. You have done what you could for me, but you could never bridge the gulf between our natures.

Some couples are not meant to be, no matter how much they love each other."

Then suddenly Irunnu felt he might collapse with grief, for the beautiful young woman, lovely Waleker, vanished before his eyes.

But there on the tree trunk, a spider was busy weaving her web.

Xibalba

K'iche' (Maya) tradition

Two brothers passed
through many dangers:
the jaguars, the bats,
a house like a glacier.
The lords of Xibalba
wanted them to lose;
to secure their defeat,
they tried every ruse.
But the brothers were brave
and clever and calm:
the Hero Twins won
there in Xibalba.

Hunahpu and Ixbalanque had defeated the lords of the underworld in their first game of ball and passed the test of the House of Darkness. However, the dark lords did not recognize the boys' triumph. To crush them as they had done with their father and uncle, Hun and Vucub, they forced the twins into the other test houses of Xibalba, the Realm of Fright.

The boys entered the so-called House of Blades, where countless knives hovered, ready to slice them to ribbons. But Hunahpu and Ixbalanque spoke to the blades, promising that the meat of hunted animals would forever be theirs. Hearing this oath, the knives lowered their points and respected the life of the brothers.

The next day, the lords of Xibalba frowned to see the boys leave as if nothing had happened, and they said to one another, "They will not emerge so easily from the House of Cold. Let us take them there at once."

This trial was a house made entirely of ice, where the cold felt unbearable. But the brothers conjured up pine torches that warmed the air and melted the ice. Very early in the morning they stepped out, opening the door of watery slush on their own.

"How is it possible?" roared the lords of Xibalba. "How have you not died yet? Guards, take them at once to the House of Jaguars. Those beasts will tear them apart and crush their bones. At last we will triumph!"

The House of Jaguars reeked of the big cats. Seeing the brothers, the spotted predators showed their fangs, preparing to leap at their throats.

"Jaguar brothers," said Ixbalanque, "don't waste your time. There's something better you can do than devour a couple of twins."

As he spoke, Hunahpu conjured up hundreds of bones, which showered down on the animals. The jaguars began to gnaw them with glee. Outside the house, the Xibalbans assumed the bones they heard being chewed and crunched were those of Hunahpu and Ixbalanque.

They were sorely surprised when the next morning the brothers exited the House of Jaguars without a single scratch. They were then sent to the House of Fire, but they left without a single burn, not even one scorched strand of hair.

"They cannot possibly escape alive from the House of Bats!" shouted the angry lords of Xibalba.

And they pushed the twins into a cave full of bats.

"This time, the night will be long and dangerous, Hunahpu," said Ixbalanque.

"You're right, Brother," said Hunahpu. "Why don't we sleep inside our blowguns? That way we'll be safe."

So they magically made the bamboo tubes bigger, climbed inside, and spent a quiet night in the midst of the man-killing bats. As the hours passed, Hunahpu decided to peek out of the blowgun to see if dawn had arrived. At that precise moment, one of the bats bit off his head with a single, ferocious bite.

"Hunahpu's dead!" Ixbalanque grieved. "But I'm still alive, so we're only half defeated."

The lords of Xibalba celebrated with great laughter. They took the head of Hunahpu and set it in the middle of the court to be used as a ball.

Then Ixbalanque summoned all the animals to help him resurrect Hunahpu. And Hurakan, Heart of Sky, who made this whole story happen, also came to his call. The coati brought a nice round squash, the size of the boys' heads, and everyone worked together to perfect the disguise, setting it on Hunahpu's shoulders. When the sun was high in the sky, the two brothers joked, confident they would beat the Xibalbans.

"Let me do the work," said Ixbalanque to Hunahpu, who was trying to keep the squash balanced on his neck. "You just focus on taking care of yourself. You're a little weak from your recent change of head. I'll let you know when it's time. Then we can defeat these tricky lords of Xibalba and avenge the death of our father and our uncle."

Ixbalanque called a rabbit and whispered some instructions in his ear. The rabbit jumped to show he understood, and the brothers headed to the ball court.

Those of Xibalba were shocked to see Hunahpu with a head on his shoulders. "But your head is there on the court!" they shouted.

Ixbalanque disagreed. "No. You're so gullible. That's just a ball in the shape of his head. Ready?"

The match began. First the lords of the underworld threw Hunahpu's real head, which they intended to use as a ball. Ixbalanque hit it with a leather-padded hip, sending it flying toward one of the gaps at the edge of the court, where the rabbit was hidden. As the gruesome ball bounced off the court, the rabbit started to hop away into the distance as fast as he could.

The Xibalbans believed the rabbit was the ball, so off they went, chasing it into the nearby fields. Meanwhile, Ixbalanque found his brother's head at the edge of the court, swapping it with the round squash the coati had brought.

The rabbit disappeared, and when the lords of Xibalba returned, Hunahpu was holding the disguised squash in his hands. "Found it!" he called.

The Xibalbans were filled with dread, suspecting the truth.

Hunahpu and Ixbalanque had regained their strength. Striking with an elbow, Ixbalanque slammed the squash against the hard surface of the ball court. It burst open, sending seeds flying everywhere.

The lords of the underworld were speechless and afraid. The two brothers from the surface world had passed, one by one, the terrible tests of Xibalba.

Xolotl

Nahua tradition

If you see some corn
with two tasseled stalks,
or a cute axolotl
that swims among frogs,
or a double maguey
in the open field,

you'll know that Xolotl
just cannot sit still.
He hides, he escapes,
he hides once again.
Why is he running?
He's afraid of the wind.

When the gods gathered in Teotihuacan to create the sun and the moon, when Nanahuatzin and Tecuciztecatl had sacrificed themselves, overcoming their fear of death to become the great lights of the cosmos, the deities realized that they also had to create movement. For neither the sun nor the moon budged from the horizon. They seemed fixed in place.

Then, one by one, the gods threw themselves into the bonfire they had lit in the great square of Teotihuacan. Ehecatl, god of wind, made sure they complied. His task would be to gather their divine essence and send it blowing at the horizon, setting sun and moon in motion.

Every god obeyed: Huitzilopochtli and Tezcatlipoca, Macuilxochitl and Xochiquetzal, Coatlicue and Xochipilli . . .

All of them sacrificed themselves except one, whose fear of death was greater than the divine will to create the new life.

It was Xolotl, double of Quetzalcoatl, who could take the form of a dog. He bore the sacred sign of movement tattooed on his arms and legs, the ollin needed to start the new age. But he fled, unwilling to die. Ehecatl followed.

Ah, Xolotl! He reached the earth, thinking himself safe. But what fear he felt when he saw his executioner arrive as a whirlwind! Again he ran, flew, fought for his life. At last he hid among the cornfields, taking the form of a corn plant with a double stalk, which the Nahuas now call "xolotl" in his honor, because he is the double of the Feathered Serpent.

In spite of his disguise, the god of the air found him. As his executioner prepared to sacrifice Xolotl, the divine dog managed to escape again. He then hid in a field, disguising himself as a doubled maguey. Now the Nahuas call the plant "mexolotl," for "me-" means "maguey" in their tongue, and xolotl is a double.

Even disguised as a doubled maguey, his features hidden and his movement tattoo covered in green, he was found by the god of air, his executioner. The elusive god morphed once more, plunging into a lagoon and becoming a curious creature the Nahuas call an "axolotl," as "a-" means "water," acquiring three pairs of gills that fanned out like fringes from the base of his head. Able to breathe on land and underwater, he could better hide from his cruel stalker. However, Ehecatl found him even in this clever and small disguise.

The shy axolotl he had become could no longer escape. His eyes spotted the flint knife: a face had been painted on the blade. The air swirled around him, the trumpeting of Quetzalcoatl's conch echoed all around, and with the death of Xolotl the sun and moon began to move.

The Fifth Age had commenced.

Yaya and Yayael

Taino tradition

On the islands they say
that the fish and the sea
were born from a boy
as rude as can be.
Lord Yaya had a son
named Yayael.

One day they fought—
it did not go well.
Yaya saved the bones
in a hollow gourd,
and when it burst,
out the fish poured.

In the beginning, Yaya created every living thing. He made the earth like a circular disc, furrowed by the undulations of mountains and islands. He added caves and wells, entrances to the watery underworld. And as a ceiling the vault of the heavens, dotted with stars, and in the center the celestial well from which the hurricanes emerged.

Yaya had a son and named him Yayael. He delighted in the boy's childhood, all smiles and promises, in the dawn of his adolescence, in Yayael's resemblance to him. But very soon, Yayael came to resent his father's power. He burned with rebellious fire. All he wanted was to rise up against Yaya, reign in his place, be the supreme god.

In the midst of a heated argument in which Yayael raised his voice against his father and threatened to kill him, Yaya, afflicted and angry, said, "I order you to leave my house. Take a canoe and paddle as far as you can to another island. You will not be able to return until four moons have passed."

Yayael gnashed his teeth in anger. And during all the days of his exile, instead of calming the storm within, he stoked the fires of hatred and revenge raging in his heart.

Thus, on his return, another fight broke out between the two. Yayael raised his hand against Yaya. In a mighty outburst of anger, Yaya ended his son's life.

When he saw him dead, Yaya repented. He cried inconsolably. He suffered as he had never done. In his grief he collected Yayael's bones one by one and put them in a higuera gourd, which he hung from the ceiling of his cabin.

Days and nights went by. Yaya found no comfort. He picked up the higuera gourd to look at the bones and remember his son.

His eyes widened, full of wonder. The inside of the higuera gourd teemed with fish, so many that it overflowed. Yaya decided to eat some. Every day he consumed some more, but the fish never ran out.

At the same time, in those beginning days of the cosmos, Mother Earth—Itiba Cahubaba—gave birth to four children, two sets of twins who emerged as adults, wild and reckless. The first-born became the leader of the brothers. His name was Deminan Caracaracol.

The twins discovered what was going on at Yaya's cabin. They wanted to see the fish-filled higuera gourd with their own eyes and take some for their own dinner. One day, when Yaya was out, they took the higuera gourd from the ceiling and stared at the countless fish swimming in circles.

"Who has dared to enter my cabin?"

The brothers were startled by the voice of Yaya, who had returned earlier than they'd expected. Fearful of being killed like Yayael, the twins dropped the higuera gourd, which slammed against the hard-packed floor, bursting open.

From the shattered remains, so much water began to shoot out that the whole world was flooded. Fish of all shapes and sizes were dragged along by that vastness of water that eventually became the sea.

That is why the Taino people believe that from the bones of Yayael and the depths of Yaya's repentance, the ocean was formed, along with all the myriad creatures that inhabit its depths, countless in number, eternally renewed.

Yupanqui

Andean tradition

The Inca Yupanqui
worked very hard.
To keep up the shrines,
he traveled quite far.

One day at a fountain
he found a mirror.
The sun spoke from within,
made his destiny clearer.

Before becoming lord of Tahuantinsuyo, when he was still a prince, Yupanqui was entrusted by his father Pachacutec to visit all the huacas or shrines of the empire and make any necessary repairs.

In the vicinity of Cuzco stood the fountain of Susur-puquio. Yupanqui stopped beside it to rest. The prince was staring at the water, deep in thought, when an object fell into the fountain. It could only have fallen from the sky, as Yupanqui was alone at the fountain and no one could be seen nearby.

He picked up the object and looked it over. It was a mirror in which he saw a glowing figure. By squinting, for the light emanating from the figure blinded him, the intrigued Yupanqui made out the marvelous form of a god. Three rays emerged from the deity's head, like glowing sunbeams. Upon his head sat a llauto, or headdress, like that worn by the Inca, Yupanqui's father, emperor of Tahuantinsuyo. He wore gilded earflaps and sumptuous robes, and from his back emerged the head and claws of a jaguar. A large snake hung from his shoulders.

Yupanqui was shocked to see the figure move his lips, wanting to speak. The prince threw the mirror back into the fountain. Gripped by fear, he began to run away. But he stopped when he heard a voice in the fountain calling out his name.

"Yupanqui, my son. Do not flee. I wish you no harm. I could never hurt you."

The sound of the voice calmed Yupanqui's heart. He felt ashamed of his cowardice. Returning to the fountain, he took the mirror in his hands, setting it carefully on the ground with much reverence.

"Who are you? How do you know my name?" asked Yupanqui.

"I am Inti, the Sun. I am your father and your father's father. I am everyone's father. I can see everything. Not just what happens in Tahuantinsuyo, but the movements of the entire cosmos itself. Past and present and also future."

"What's in my future, Father Sun?" asked Yupanqui. "Will I ever become the Inca?"

"You will, no doubt," said the sun from within the mirror. "You and your descendants are destined to rule over many nations. So much land will you control that it would be impossible for you to imagine at this time. That is why the Incas should always think of me, take me into account, bow and remember me in their sacrifices, always. Always, Yupanqui, future Inca."

The sun fell silent and his figure disappeared from the mirror, together with his llauto and gold jewels, his jaguar and his snake. Yupanqui took the mirror and always kept it with him. It became his main counselor, through which he learned all he wanted to know.

When Yupanqui became Inca, the first thing he ordered was the construction of a temple to the sun god in Cuzco. In time it rose above the city, glittering with such magnificence as had never been seen before in Tahuantinsuyo, empire of the Incas.

Cemis

Taino tradition

Gods of sand,
sun and wave.
Cemis, they're called,
and honor they crave.
Should a tree quiver
when the wind doesn't blow,
there's a spirit inside—
it's a cemi, you know.
If you travel to Cuba,
Jamaica or Haiti
you will always be lucky
if you see a cemi.

In the distant past, on the islands of the Caribbean, the most numerous beings that existed were all cemis, nature spirits full of healing power. They lived between heaven and earth, between gods and men.

Time passed, the years wore on, and the cemis continued to exist in the human world, manifesting in many different ways.

When a person found their path obstructed by a tree that quivered from its roots without the wind blowing or anyone shaking it, they suspected it was a cemi. Despite the fear they might feel, they would stop and ask:

"Tree, what do you want?"

To which the tree would answer, "Bring a shaman, a behique. He will tell you who I am."

The person would comply, and the behique would come, full of respect, to ask the cemi in the tree what it wanted done with it. This communication happened through the cohoba ritual. In a vision, the behique would learn how to carve the wood of the tree to shape a new cemi. Then a house would be built for it, and men and women would show daily reverence to the spirit. In return, the cemi gave good advice that had to be interpreted. Everyone was very satisfied.

As time went by, there came to be more humans than cemis, but the spirits still managed to get the attention of mortals. Now, in the form of statues of wood, stone, mud, cotton or shell, they continue living in our world.

Some of the first cemis were the four sons of Itiba Cahubaba, Mother Earth. After bursting open the higuera gourd with Yayael's bones and creating the sea, these brothers sought a new opportunity to sate their curiosity and prove their bravery.

Guided by the eldest, Deminan Caracaracol, they decided to steal from Bayamanaco, a fire cemi, not only the secret recipe for cassava bread—cababe, most amazing food—but also the important secret of the cohoba rite.

The ritual required a powder made from the seed of an unknown tree, also a cemi. That powder was inhaled through a pipe into the nose. Doing so, Bayamanaco, the first behique, could contemplate with his eyes closed the creation of the world, the mysteries of life and death, the healing of all possible diseases.

When the brothers stole Bayamanaco's secrets, the behique, full of rage, hurled fire at the brothers, singeing their hair. Then he spewed guanguayo on Deminan Caracaracol's back. Immediately, in the place where the liquid had fallen, a hump formed.

"What?" Deminan Caracaracol cried, almost falling backward under the weight of the hump.

"We told you that Bayamanaco was a powerful cemi. You didn't care about the risk," said one of the twins.

"But relax," said another. "We already have the important secrets in our possession."

"I can't go on like this," said Deminan Caracaracol. "The hump weighs more with every passing minute."

The brothers agreed to help release him from that unexpected punishment. They retired to a cave to discuss their options.

After proposing several solutions, they decided it would be best to slice off the hump with an ax. With a mighty whack they cut their brother free. To their surprise, a huge cemi turtle emerged from the hump—beautiful Caguama.

The twins took care of the turtle, fed it and built it a home.

Many years later, the astonishing turtle Caguama would become the mother of all humans in those enchanted Caribbean lands, isles bathed by the turquoise sea and gilded each evening by the setting sun.

Zamna

Itza (Maya) tradition

A long white road
stretched toward the sea;
down it they walk,
the people of peace.
Women and children,
elders and more,
seeking a new home
down by the shore.

Most Itza have gone,
they've left without fighting.
The Toltec army
just lets them pass.
They've set out in search
of white Izamal,
following a prophet
whose name is Zamna.

When the lords of Xibalba were defeated, the effects were felt throughout the sea-ringed world. Many peoples had to emigrate from their ancestral lands. Some headed for Tollan, while others followed the flight of the birds toward the peninsula of Yucatan. These were the Itza, guided by their high priest, Zamna.

"I am the substance of the sky. I am the dew of the clouds," Zamna cryptically declared. He was not a warrior or a king attired all in gold, but a man of ideas, whose thoughts were rich with past and whose vision burgeoned with future.

A prophet, Zamna, deciphered signs that arose during his people's trek, until they came to a good and promising land. There in eastern Yucatan, Zamna sank his staff in a crack in the rocky soil to indicate that, at long last, the Itza nation had found its new home.

They believed him. For Zamna organized their lives, giving names to the new animals they encountered, pointing out local plants with healing properties, commanding the four winds to change their directions, sending scouts to behold the great sea. Hints of its existence came upon the breezes that pulled clouds along and awakened a strange nostalgia in the hearts of the Itza.

"Someday," they told one another, "we will all of us travel the paths of the sea."

Zamna tested men to decide whether they should be farmers, priests or warriors, according to their skills and knowledge. Having defined their roles, Zamna sent bands of people to found other cities: Chichen Itza to the East; to the South, Copan. They founded T'Ho to the West; and to the North, a hidden city was established to preserve the ancient books and dreams—Izamal.

Zamna ordered the construction of magnificent temples to track the passage of the stars. Beautiful pyramids, stuccoed and painted red, elegant observatories for watching the heavens. That good and generous land yielded so many fruits that no one knew hunger. Corn harvests were abundant and clear water bubbled up from wells to the delight of the Itza.

One day that same water grew clouded. One afternoon a wind filled with sandstone began to blow. One night the roar of a dark jaguar was heard in the sky. A worried time arrived, black days full of omens and sadness.

Scouts returned. An army had been sighted. Gleaming men of arms, bedecked in battle feathers, shouting with warlike voices, approached Chichen Itza.

The Toltec empire had found the route to Yucatan.

Gifted with wisdom from heaven's heart, Zamna knew that the reign of the Itza nation was at an end. Why wage war? Why destroy life and dreams? Why raze the beautiful temples, those sacred mountains? Their calculations, their buildings, would undoubtedly serve to enrich the lives of newcomers, just as human as the Itza, their shared ancestors fashioned by the gods, pilgrims like the Itza, drawn toward the place of origin, toward the sea.

The high priest spoke to his people, sharing his plan. Some Itza chose to remain and parlay with the Toltecs. Others would follow a different path.

That night, as the Toltec army camped outside the wall, Zamna drove his staff once more into the ground beside the great cenote, well of the gods.

In the morning, a broad white road stretched toward the horizon. Down its length began to walk the elderly, women, little girls and boys, brave warriors in the flower of age.

Their destination was the hidden city, Izamal.

They were the Itza people, and Zamna led them.

Transcription of Indigenous Terms

When Europeans arrived in the Americas, the clash of cultures was accompanied by a clash of languages as well. People unfamiliar with indigenous names tried to express those words with Roman letters and English, Spanish, or Portuguese sounds. As a result, especially in Latin American countries, indigenous words have been transcribed in peculiar ways, using diacritics (accents and so forth) that squeeze the names into the rules of those colonizing languages.

We have decided in this book to remove those marks (most of which are meaningless to readers of English, anyway).

Of course, some Native nations have taken back the transcription of their languages. That practice often includes diacritics used in ways particular to those peoples. We have often elected not to use those, either, for the sake of consistency and because readers will for the most part not understand the significance of the marks.

Ultimately, the mission of this collection is to make a broader readership familiar with vital sacred stories that have endured for millennia throughout the Americas. While not a perfect system, we trust our transcription decisions will promote greater understanding.

Pronunciation Guide

Indigenous languages were transcribed after the European conquest using Roman letters and the spelling conventions of colonizers' languages. As a result, it is difficult to generalize pronunciation rules for *all* of the Native words in this book. However, some broad, basic tendencies are summarized below. Approximate pronunciations can be found in the glossary.

Vowels
a   as in "father"
e   as in "bet"
i   as in "police"
o   as in "no"
u   as in "flute"

Diphthongs (vowel combinations)
ai   like the "y" in "my"
au   like "ow" in "cow"
ei   like the "ay" in "hay"
eu   a blend of "e" of "bet" and "u" of flute

ia like the "ya" of "yard"
ie like the "ye" of "yellow"
io like the "yo" of "yodel"
iu like "you"
ua like the "wa" in "want"
ue like the "whe" in "where"
ui like "we"

Consonants

b as in "baby"
c like "k" before "a," "o" and "u";
   like "s" before "e" and "i"
d as in "dog" at the beginning of
   a word; like the "th" in "that"
   elsewhere
f as in "four"
g like the "g" in "go" before "a,"
   "o" and "u"; like "h" before "e"
   and "i" in Latin America
h for languages in Latin America,
   usually silent
j like "j" in "jam," except for Latin
   America, where it is like "h," but
   harsher
l as in "like"
m as in "moon"

n as in "no"
ñ roughly like the "ni" in "onion"
p as in "pet"
r like the "dd" in the American
   pronunciation of "ladder"
s as in "see"
t as in "ten"
v like "b" in "baby"
x like "sh" in "she"
y as in "yes" (though pronounced
   "eu" in Guarani)
z like "s" in "see"

Digraphs (two letters always written together)

ch   as in "check"
cu/uc "kw" as in "queen" (primarily
       Nahuatl)
hu/uh like "w" in "we"
ll   like "y" in "yes" (Spanish
       only)
qu   like "k" in "key"
rr   a "rolled r" (Spanish only)
tl   roughly like the "ttle" in
       "bottle"
tz   like the "ts" in "cats"

Note also that most words are stressed on the next-to-the-last syllable:
Hapunda—ha/PUN/da
Citlalli—ci/TLAL/li
Tezcatlipoca—tez/ca/tli/PO/ca
Quetzalcoatl—que/tzal/CO/atl

A Quick Guide to Cultures

Alutiiq (Sugpiaq)—interrelated Native tribes whose ancestral homelands include the southern coast of Alaska and the Kodiak Archipelago.

Andean—various Native peoples (including the Atacamak, Aymara, Quechua, Uru, and Diaguita) living in the Andes Mountains of South America, united under the Incas before the Spanish conquest.

Bribri—Native clans living in the mountains and islands of what is now southern Costa Rica and northern Panama.

Cabecar—a Native group living in modern Costa Rica, closely related to the Bribri and sharing many of the same beliefs and customs.

Guarani—a South American indigenous people living throughout modern Paraguay, Argentina, Brazil, Bolivia, and Uruguay.

Hopi—a Native American tribe living mainly in Hopitutskwa, their sovereign ancestral land in what is now the state of Arizona.

Inuit—a group of culturally interrelated Native peoples (principally the Inuit, Inuvialuit, Kalaallit Inuit, Inupiat and Yup'ik) living in parts of Canada, Greenland, Russia and the US.

Mapuche—a culturally and linguistically interrelated group of Native peoples living in modern Chile, Argentina, and Patagonia.

Maya—a collective term for the Native peoples of what is now southern Mexico, Guatemala, Belize, El Salvador and Honduras. Among the many individual groups are the Itza, K'iche', Mopan, Tzotzil and Yucatec.

Muisca—a Native people living in the highlands of what is now Colombia; at the time of the Spanish conquest, theirs was the greatest civilization in the Americas after the Incas, Nahuas and Maya.

Nahua—a collective term for Native peoples interconnected through culture and language, the largest indigenous group in Mexico and second largest group in El Salvador. Historically important groups such as the Toltecs and the Mexica (often known as Aztecs) were Nahuas.

Niitsitapi—also Blackfoot Confederacy or Siksikaitsitapi. A group of First Nation Bands and Native American tribes living in modern Canada and Montana, commonly known as Blackfeet.

Ojibwe—a group of First Nation / Native Anishinaabe people of Canada and US Midwest, one of the most populous indigenous group north of the Rio Grande. The story "Gichi-manidoo" most likely comes from the Michigan area.

Oceti Sakowin—also Sioux. First Nation / Native American peoples of modern

Canada and the US. The Great Sioux Nation is a traditional structure that includes multiple Lakota and Dakota tribes into a single cultural group.

Selk'nam (Ona)—an indigenous people in what is now southern Argentina and Chile, including the Tierra del Fuego islands. Though they were believed "extinct" during the late 20th century, thousands of Ona people live at present in Argentina.

Taino—an indigenous people of the Caribbean, the first to be encountered by Europeans, originally inhabiting what is now Cuba, Hispaniola, Jamaica, Puerto Rico, The Bahamas and the northern Lesser Antilles. Despite Spanish claims that they had died out, people of Taino ancestry live throughout the Caribbean and the US today.

Wayuu—an Indigenous people living on the Guajira Peninsula that makes up the northernmost part of Colombia and northwest Venezuela.

Wixarika—widely known as Huichol people, the Wixarika are an indigenous people living in the Sierra Madre Occidental range in the modern Mexican states of Nayarit, Jalisco, Zacatecas, and Durango.

The map on the facing page shows the approximate locations of all the cultures represented in this book.

GREENLAND

Inuit

a (Sugpiac)

NORTH
AMERICA

Niitsitapi (Blackfoot)

Ojibwe

Oceti Sakowin
(Sioux)

NORTH
PACIFIC
OCEAN

NORTH
ATLANTIC
OCEAN

Hopi

Nahua

Wixarika

Maya

Taino

Cabecar
Bribri

Wayuu

Muisca

SOUTH
AMERICA

Guarani

Andean

SOUTH
PACIFIC
OCEAN

SOUTH
ATLANTIC
OCEAN

Mapuche

Selk'nam (Ona)

Glossary

Aakulujjuusi (ah koo looj JOO see)—one of the first two men in Inuit tradition

Acoyanapa (ah koh yah NAH pah)—Andean llama shepherd

Alux (ah LOOSH)—an elf in Maya tradition

Antu (AHN too)—Mapuche god of the sun

Arami (ah rah MEE)—wife of a Guarani cacique

Ayvu (ah eu VOO)—soul-word of Guarani god Ñamandu

Aztlan (AST lahn)—original homeland of the Mexica

Bacabs (BAH kahbs)—Maya gods who hold up the sky

Bacata (bah kah TAH)—now Bogotá, a region in modern Colombia

Bachue (bah choo WEY)—the blue-eyed goddess of water in Muisca tradition.

Bayamanaco (bah yah mah NAH koh)—the first behique or shaman in Taino tradition

Bochica (boh CHEE kah)—prophet and teacher of the Muisca

Busiraco (boo see RAH koh)—in Muisca tradition, an evil dragon that feeds on fire

Calcu (KAL koo)—sorcerer in Mapuche tradition

Ce Acatl Topiltzin (se AH kaht toh peelt SEEN)—human incarnation of Quetzalcoatl
    king of Tollan

Cemi (SHE mee)—minor god in Taino tradition

Centzonhuitznahuah (sent son weets NAH wah)— Nahua gods of the southern stars

Chibchachum (cheeb CHAH choom)—Muisca god who protects their lands and waters

Chiminigagua (chee mee nee GAH wah)—supreme Muisca god

Chuquillanto (choo kee YAHN toh)—most beautiful of the ñustas in Andean tradition

Cihuacoatl (see wah KO aht)—Nahua goddess of motherhood

Cihuateteo (see wah teh TEH oh)—the fierce spirits of Nahua women who died in childbirth

Cipactonal (see pak TOH nal)—the first man in Nahua tradition

Coatlicue (koh aht LEEK weh)—Nahua goddess who gave birth to Huitzilopochtli

Coyolxauhqui (koh yol SHAW kee)—Nahua goddess of the moon

Coatrisque (kwah TREES kyeh)—assistant of Guabancex who causes floods

Cuzco (COOS koh)—capital city of the Incas

Deminan Caracaracol (deh MEE nan KAH rah kah rah KOL)—Taino demigod, son of
    Mother Earth

Ehecatl (eh HEH kaht)—Nahua god of the wind

Gichi-manidoo (GEE chee MAH nee doh)—"the Great Spirit," Ojibwe creator god

Guabancex (wah BAHN ses)—cemi of hurricanes

Guabonito (wah boh NEE toh)—cemi of healing

ahayona (wah hah YOH nah)—legendary Taino hero

atauba (wah TAW bah)—assistant of Guabancex who makes lightning and thunder

atavita (wah tah VEE tah)—lake in Colombia and Muisca kingdom on its shores

owenh (HOH wen)—minor Selk'nam gods

uitzilopochtli (weet see loh POHCH tlee)—Nahua god of the sun and war

unahpu (hoo NAH poo)—one of the Maya hero twins who defeat the Lords of Xibalba

un Batz (hoon BAHTS)—one of the sons of Hun Hunahpu

un Chowen (hoon choh WEN)—brother of Hun Batz

un Hunahpu (hoon hoo NAH poo)—minor god of corn; father to not only Hun Batz and
        Hun Chowen, but also the hero twins Hunahpu and Ixbalanque.

urakan (hoo rah KAHN)—Taino and Maya god of storms, also known as Heart of Sky

sawu (ee SAH woo)—Coyote, trickster figure of the Hopi

ıti (EEN tee)—Andean sun god

palnemohuani (ee pal neh moh WAH nee)—"Giver of Life," title of Ometeotl

zamna (eet SAHM nah)—Maya creator god

xbalanque (eesh bah LAHN keh)— one of the Maya hero twins who defeat the Lords
        of Xibalba

x Chebel Yax (eesh CHEH bel YASH)—Maya creator goddess

xchel (eesh CHEL)—Maya goddess of the moon

xmucane (eesh moo KAH neh)—mother of Hun Hunahpu and Vucub Hunahpu

xquic (eesh KEEK)—daughter of one of the Lords of Xibalba; mother of the hero twins
        Hunapu and Ixbalanque

ztaccihuatl (ees tahk SEE waht)—Nahua princess who becomes a dormant volcano
        after death

Jakaira (ya kah ee RAH)—Guarani god of mist and smoke

Jasy Jatere (jah SEU jah teh REH)—fragment of the moon

Kaila (kah EE lah)—the Inuit god of heaven

Kanek (kah NEK)—prince of Chichen Itza

Karai (kah rah EE)—Guarani god of fire and sunlight

Kauyumari (kah oo yoo MAH ri)—"Blue Deer," a Huichol deity

K'awil (KAH weel)—Maya god of lightning and magic

Kookyangwso'wuuti (koo kyahngw soh woo tee)—Spider Grandmother, Old Spider
        Woman, one of two Hopi sister deities

Kukulkan (koo kool KAHN)—"Feathered Serpent," Maya creator god (known as
        Quetzalcoatl to the Nahuas)

Kuyen (koo YEN)—Mapuche goddess of the moon

Llorona (yoh ROH nah)—a wailing spirit with roots in Nahua tradition

Magaju (mah GAH joo)—a young Sioux woman who became the rain

Mayab (MAH yahb)—the Yucatan peninsula

Mayahuel (ma YAH wel)—Nahua goddess of maguey plants

Mexica (meh SHEE kah)—a nation of Nahua people

Mexitli (meh SHEET lee)—man who led the Mexica people out of Aztlan

Mictecacihuatl (meek teh kah SEE what)—goddess of Mictlan

Mictlan (MEEKT lahn)—Nahua land of the dead

Mictlanteuctli (meekt lahn TEKT lee)—god of Mictlan

Miohpoisiks (mee oh PO ee siks)—Blackfoot name for the Pleiades

Mixcoatl (meesh KOH aht)—"Cloud Serpent," demi-god of the hunt, father of Quetzalcoa

Moneta (moh neh TAH)—a holy man and hero of Muisca tradition

Muy'ingwa (muee EENG woo)—Hopi germination spirit

Nahual (NAH wal)—an animal soul or double in Nahua tradition

Naj Tunich (nah too NEECH)—holy site in the Maya Mountains

Nanahuatzin (nah nah WAHT seen)—Nahua god of the sun

Ñamandu (nyah mahn DOO)—supreme god in Guarani tradition

Ñanderu Mba'ekua (nyan deh ROO em bah eh KWAH)—Guarani god who helped forr.
      the first goddess.

Ñandesy (nyan deh SEU)—the first goddess in Guarani tradition

Ñustas (NYOOS tahs)—angelic maidens consecrated to the Sun in Andean tradition

Omecihuatl (oh meh SEE waht) —the female half of the Nahua Dual God, Ometeotl

Ometeotl (oh meh TEH oht) —the Nahua Dual God, union of female and male in one
      two-spirit being

Ometeuctli (oh meh TEKT lee) —the male half of the Nahua Dual God, Ometeotl

Oxomoco (oh shoh MOH koh)—the first woman in Nahua tradition

Pachacutec (pah chah KOO tek)—Incan prince

Pacha Kamaq (PAH chah KAH mahk)—Andean creator god

Panaq (PAH nahk)—young Sugpiaq hunter who tries to kill the legendary white bear

Piltzinteuctli (peelt seen TEKT lee)—"Beloved Young Prince," first child born to the first
      human couple in Nahua tradition

Popocatepetl (poh poh kah TEH pet)—Nahua warrior who becomes an active volcano

Pu-Am (poo AHM)—the Mapuche creator god

Py'aguasu (peu AH gwa SOO)—"Great Heart," Guarani god of words, good conduct and divine love

ilertetang (kah ee ler TEH tang)—Inuit goddess of weather; lover of Sedna

t'sqaq (KAHT skahk)—Sugpiaq hunter who becomes a white bear

etzalcoatl (ket sal KOH aht)—"Feathered Serpent," Nahua creator god

uilaztli (kee LAHST lee)—another name for Cihuacoatl

mac (REE mahk)—a speaking statue in Andean tradition

k Nikte (SAHK neek TEH)—princess of Mayapan

edna (SED nah)—Inuit goddess of the sea

bo (SEE boh)—creator god in Cabecar and Bribri tradition

ramena (see rah MEH nah)—priestess of the Muisca god Bochica

orkula (sor KOO lah)—shaman in Cabecar and Bribri tradition

aawa (TAH wah)—chief Hopi spirit

aguapacac (tah wah PAH kahk)—one of Viracocha's assistants, who rebels against
the god

ahuantinsuyo (tah wahn teen SOO yoh)—name of the Inca homeland

amoanchan (tah moh AHN chahn)—Nahua paradise

emaukel (teh MAW kel)—Selk'nam creator god

enochtitlan (teh nohch TEET lahn)—capital of the Triple Alliance, commonly known
as the Aztec Empire

eotihuacan (teh oh tee WAH kahn)—divine city where the Nahua gods made the sun
and moon

epeyollotl (tey peh YOL loht)—"Heart of Mountain," the jaguar form of Tezcatlipoca

euacciztecatl (tek sees TEK aht)—Nahua god of the moon

ezcatlipoca (tes kaht lee POH kah)—"Smoking Mirror," Nahua god of storms and
chaos, brother of Quetzalcoatl

Tlaloc (TLAH lohk)—Nahua god of storms, ruling over the paradise of Tlalocan

Tloqueh Nahuaqueh (TLOH keh nah WAH keh)—"Lord of the Near and the Nigh," title
of Ometeotl

Trempulkalwe (trem pool KAL weh)—divine whales in Mapuche tradition that guide souls

Tupa (too PAH)—Guarani god of creation

Turey (TOO rey)—Taino god of the sky

Tzitzimimeh (tsee tsee MEE meh)—fierce Nahua star goddesses

Uirapuru (wee rah poo ROO)—Guarani warrior, transformed into a bird

Ulil (oo LEEL)—prince of Uxmal

Utahu (oo TAH hoo)—a young Sioux man who was transformed into an oak

Uumarnituq (ooh mar NEE took)—one of the first two men in Inuit tradition; becomes pregnant and transforms into a woman

Vichama (vee CHAH mah)—son of the sun god in Andean tradition

Viracocha (vee rah KOH chah)—Andean creator god

Vucub Hunahpu (WOO koob hoo NAH poo)—brother of Hun Hunahpu, his main companion and helper

Wakangli (wah KONG lee)—Sioux god of lightning

Waleker (wah LEH kehr)—Wayuu spider who takes the form of a human girl

Wekufe (weh KOO feh)—harmful spirits in Mapuche tradition

Xalpen (HAL pen)—monster in Selk'nam tradition

Xibalba (shee bal BAH)—the dark Maya underworld

Xipe Totec (SHEE peh TOH tek)—Nahua god who rules the East

Xiuhnel (SHEEW nel)—a Mexica hunter

Xochipilli (shoh chee PEEL lee)—"Flower Prince," Nahua god of flowers

Xochiquetzal (shoh chee KET sal)—"Flower Beauty," Nahua goddess of flowers

Xolotl (SHOH loht)—the nahual or double of Quetzalcoatl

Yaya (YAH yah)—Taino creator god

Yayael (yah YAH el)—rebellious son of Yaya

Yupanqui (yoo PAHN kee)—Incan prince, son of Pachacutec

Zamna (SAHM nah)—priest and leader of the Itza, a Maya people

Zipa (SEE pah)—the title of the Muisca ruler

Bibliography

Benítez, Fernando. *Los indios de México*. Tomo III. Mexico City: Ediciones Era, 1970.

Bierhorst, John. *Codex Chimalpopoca: The Text in Nahuatl with a Glossary and Grammatical Notes*. Tucson: The University of Arizona Press, 1992.

Bierhorst, John. *History and Mythology of the Aztecs: The Codex Chimalpopoca*. Tucson: The University of Arizona Press, 1992.

Bierhorst, John. *The Mythology of South America*. United Kingdom, Oxford University Press, 2002.

Bowles, David. *Feathered Serpent, Dark Heart of Sky: Myths of Mexico*. El Paso: Cinco Puntos Press, 2018.

Christenson, Allen J. *Popol Vuh: The Sacred Book of the Maya*. Norman, OK: University of Oklahoma Press, 2012.

De la Garza Camino, Mercedes. *Literatura Maya*. Caracas: Fundación Biblioteca Ayacucho, 1980.

az del Castillo, Bernal. [1585] *Historia verdadera de la conquista de la Nueva España*. Mexico City: Editorial Porrúa, 1976.

·does, Richard and Alfonso Ortiz. *American Indian Myths and Legends*. New York: Knopf Doubleday Publishing Group, 2013.

scalada Salvo, Rosita. *Myths and Legends: A Journey around the Guaraní Lands*. Argentina: Editorial Universitaria de Misiones, 2004.

aribay Kintana, Ángel M. *Teogonía e historia de los mexicanos: tres opúsculos del siglo xvi*. Mexico City: Editorial Porrúa, 1965.

older, F.A. "A Kadiak Island Story: The White-Faced Bear" in *The Journal of American Folklore* Vol. 20, No. 79. Boston and New York: Houghton, Mifflin and Company, Oct. - Dec., 1907.

ansen, Maarten and Gabina Aurora Pérez Jiménez. Paisajes sagrados: códices y arqueología de Ñuu Dzaui, en Itinerarios Vol. 8. Warsaw: Instituto de Estudios Ibéricos e Iberoamericanos, 2008.

ópez Austin. *Los mitos del tlacuache: caminos de la mitología mesoamericana*. *Alianza Estudio: Antropología*. Mexico City: UNAM, 1996.

León-Portilla, Miguel and Earl Shorris. *In the Language of Kings: An Anthology of Mesoamerican Literature, Pre-Columbian to the Present*. New York: W.W. Norton & Company, 2002.

Markman, Roberta H. and Peter T. Markman. *The Flayed God: The Mesoamerican Mythological Tradition*. San Francisco: Harper Collins, 1992.

Margery Peña, Enrique, and Sánchez Avendaño, Carlos. *Estudios de mitología comparada indoamericana*. Costa Rica, Editorial de la Universidad de Costa Rica, 2003.

Miller, Mary and Karl Taube. *An Illustrated Dictionary of the Gods and Symbols of Ancient Mexico and the Maya*. London: Thames & Hudson, 1993.

Mitchell, Judy, et al. *Handbook of Native American Mythology*. United Kingdom: ABC-CLIO, 2004.

Peniche Barrera, Roldán. *El libro de los fantasmas mayas*. Mexico City: Maldonado Editores, Biblioteca Básica del Mayab, 1992.

Sahagún, Bernadino de. *Florentine Codex: General History of the Things of New Spain*, Books I-XII, 2nd edition. Trans. and Ed. Charles E. Dibble and Arthur J. O. Anderson. 12 volumes (1950-1969). Santa Fe: University of Utah, 2012.

Stephens, John Lloyd. *Incidents of Travel in Yucatán*, Volumes I and II. New York: Harper & Brothers, 1858.

Sullivan, Thelma. *Scattering of Jades: Stories, Poems, and Prayers of the Aztecs*. Ed. Timothy J. Knab. Tucson: University of Arizona Press, 1994.

Wolfson, Evelyn. *Inuit Mythology*. Berkeley Heights, NJ; Enslow Pub., 2001.

Some Notes on This Book's Production

The art for the jacket and interiors was created digitally by Amanda Mijangos, some pieces begun as pencil sketches. The text was set by Semadar Megged in Bodoni Egyptian Pro, a typeface designed by Nick Shinn for Shinntype in 2010, building off of the family first introduced by Giambattista Bodoni in the late 1700s. The book was printed on 140 gsm Golden Sun woodfree FSC™-certified paper and bound in China.

Special thanks for their consultation to Romy Natalia Goldberg, Jorge Baracutei Estevez (Cacike of Higuayagua Taino), Delana L. Smith (Red Lake Nation), Linsey McMurrin (Leech Lake Band of Ojibwe), Virgil Edwards (Blackfeet), the Sisseton-Wahpeton Oyate Dakotah Language Institute, and Jana Schmieding (Lakota Sioux).

Production was supervised by Leslie Cohen and Freesia Blizard
Book jacket and interiors designed by Semadar Megged
Edited by Nick Thomas

LEVINE QUERIDO